INTRODUCTION

Sweet Teacher Friends,

We are excited to begin this journey through Galatians 5:22-23 with you. Before we get too far, there are a few things we would like you to know.

First, allow us to introduce ourselves for those who do not know us.

Bonnie was born and raised in a rural Georgia town. Studying at Southeastern Baptist Theological Seminary brought her to North Carolina. During her time at seminary, she studied Women's Ministry, but God had a slightly different plan for her to teach in a local kindergarten classroom.

Bethany was born and raised in a small town in Virginia. She studied Communications and Women's Ministry at Liberty University. From 2007-2016, she was living the city life in Florida. In 2016, she moved to North Carolina to teach middle and high school English. Though English is a passion, Bible trumps even her love for grammar. And y'all, that's big!

Secondly, let us address how to use this study.

We will be using the English Standard Version throughout this study. When we ask you questions or provide fill-in-the-blank sections, the ESV will help you to best answer these questions and fill in the blanks. If you do not have an ESV Bible, you can use the online version found at www.esv.org.

Throughout the study, you will find QR codes that link to worship songs or videos that correspond with our lessons. Each QR code comes with a bit.ly link that will lead you to the same song or video in case you'd rather just use good ol' Google. If you go that route, just type the bit.ly into your browser, and it'll take you there. If you need help using the QR codes, check out the next page for step-by-step instructions.

Each week, we have provided you with Scripture to memorize as well. We both firmly believe in the power of hiding God's Word in our hearts. Our favorite way to memorize Scripture is to write them on index cards or sticky notes and pop them on our mirrors, in our cars, and in our classrooms - wherever we will see it the most. You won't regret spending a few moments each day hiding God's precious Words in your heart!

Lastly, you may notice some grammar baubles.

While Bethany LOVES her some grammar, we have also chosen to make our study conversational. So, yes, that means we've started sentences with conjunctions. We've ended sentences with prepositions. We've purposely used fragments in places. Bonnie thinks that's SO okay! Bethany says it's okay because as she tells her students, "If you know the rule and know you're breaking it and have a reason for breaking it, it's permissible." (Just don't apply that to life, please. 😂)

Our prayer is that this study will challenge you as we learn how to live **#thefruitedlyfe** 😎 together so that everything we do points to Jesus and draws others to Him.

Bethany   *Bonnie Kathryn*

HOW TO USE QR CODES

TEACHERS IN THE Word

We both use QR codes in our classroom. QR codes are a fun way to make learning tech-based and interactive. Bethany uses QR codes for self-check in her centers. It helps her to avoid having 20 questions during an activity. It is a great way for students to self-assess. Bonnie uses QR codes for write-the-room activities, listening-to-reading activities, and to show how-to videos for handwriting. She begins the school year teaching her five-year-olds about QR codes and how to use them on the class iPads. We believe that if Bonnie's kindergarten students can use a QR code reader, so can you!

 You will want to download a FREE QR code reader app on your iPad, iPhone, or Android phone. Do not pay for one. There are SO many free options that work well. If you find that one is acting quirky, delete it, and pick another free option. If you have a newly updated iPhone and/or iPad, open your camera and hold it over the code. The weblink will pop up on your screen.

 Open your newly downloaded QR code reader app. You will need to give it access to your camera. It will prompt you.

 The app will have a square box that you will hold over the QR code. It should scan immediately, and it will take you to the QR code link. Essentially, the QR code links to different webpages. Throughout this study, our QR codes are linked to videos.

 Try it out here:

SOCIAL MEDIA CHALLENGES

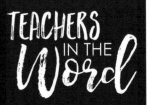

We have created weekly social media challenges for you, so we can interact on social media. Please share your challenge pictures in our Teachers in the Word Facebook group or on Instagram using the hashtags **#fruited** or **#thefruitedlyfe.** Please remember in order for us to see posts on Instagram, you will need a public account.

 **1** Post a picture of you and your teaching bestie. Bonus points if you are doing the study with your teaching bestie.

 **2** Make a fruit dessert, share the recipe, and give it to someone you love. Post a picture of any or all parts of this challenge.

 **3** Post a picture of something that brings you joy.

 **4** Post a picture of a coloring page you have completed in the study.

 **5** Post a picture of a random act of kindness.

 **6** Post of a picture of someone who is exhibits faithfulness or a video of you describing 3 ways God has been faithful to you.

 **7** Fill out the **#fruited** Instagram template and post your responses. You can grab the template on www.teachersintheword.com/fruited

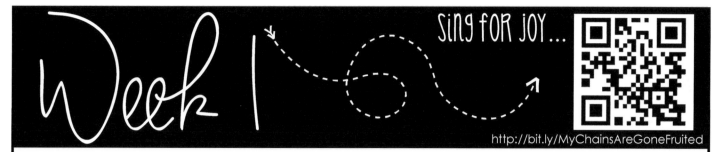

SCRIPTURE MEMORY: "He is like a tree planted by streams of water that yields its fruit in its season and its leaf does not wither. In all that he does, he prospers." Psalm 1:3

Have you ever had a student that reminds you of yourself? Like spittin' image...are you sure we aren't related somehow? I, Bethany, have had several like that. Some are so in love with literature and **#allthingsgrammar** that it makes my heart skip a beat. Some, however, share my uber perfectionistic ways, and for that I cringe and beg them not to let it get the best of them...because let's face it, perfectionism ain't always a good thing. 😊

One such student I will never forget. I was assigning the first dialectical journal entry of the year. This first one was the basic summary and question asking or comment making entry where I ask them to choose two - T-W-O - sections or pages or chapters to summarize. Then, they ask a handful of questions or make a handful of critical thinking comments that are not answered or discussed within the portion of text they read.

Well, dear child of mine - or shall I say, twin of mine - stays after class and says, "Two, Miss Fleming? Are you sure I don't need to do all the chapters? I can't ask like 20 questions instead of a handful? I mean I really don't think I can stop myself. Like I really need to do it all!" To which I replied, "No, darling. What you need to do is trust that me, your teacher, is telling you exactly what you need to do. You don't need to do more than I've asked you to do. I know what is best for this assignment because I know why I'm having you do the assignment. Trust me."

Because I've always taught in Christian schools, it's easy for me to tie in Christian principles. This student happened to be a rather strong Christian, so I looked at her and said, "Sweetheart, do you know that the people in Galatia were doing this with salvation? They were trying to add things to the salvation requirements for the Gentiles." I then asked her, "Do we need to do anything extra to earn God's love and His salvation?" She quietly shook her head no. "While this assignment is in NO way as valuable as salvation, you're trying to do the same thing. You aren't trusting that I know what's best for you in this situation." With that, she looked at me and said, "You're right. I'm only going to do two."

The next day, lo and behold, I saw only two little summaries and a handful of questions.

We're going to see this week how the one major controversy in Galatia had everything to do with not trusting the authority, but instead, trying to override the authority and add to what they said was necessary. How very dangerous when the authority they were trying to override was God Himself. Yikes! 😮

4

Imagine getting a text, an email, or a letter from someone you know well but haven't seen for a bit. It begins with a normal greeting - the "Hey" or "Dear [insert your name]" - but then, once you get past the greeting, you are smacked with quite the angry words. Unexpected for sure! Well...welcome to Galatians. That's how Paul begins this letter. Yikes, right?! 😮

We want you to see this for yourself. Open your Bible and read Galatians 1:6.

What emotion does Paul use to describe himself as he expresses his feelings regarding the Galatians' choice to turn away from the Gospel he preached to them?

Paul was _____

It is fun to look at how different versions of the Bible translate words from the original Greek language. If you want to do this for yourself, we suggest using the YouVersion app or something similar. Take a moment to look at some of the different versions we found interesting:

Version	1:6
ESV	astonished
CSB, NIV	amazed
KJV	marvel
MSG	I can't believe your fickleness
AMP	astonished and extremely irritated
NLT	shocked

Have you ever had someone do something that made you astonished, amazed, shocked, or extremely irritated? What about in your classroom? Have you ever experienced these emotions? Can everybody say, "Yes and Amen?!" Think about that time or write about it in the box below.

Just for fun, Paul was like the teacher in this video. Be ready to laugh...we know you have felt this way too! 😅

http://bit.ly/paulsclass

We often tell our students things like "Who you hang out with is who you will become," or "Show me your five closest friends, and I'll show you your future," or "What you listen to and watch influences how you think and behave." The Galatians were finding out these truths the hard way. Don't we often learn like that, too? It's like we have to fall sometimes before the truth hits us. **#sadreality** 😦

The Galatians had allowed some people into their sphere of influence that weren't preaching the truth. They had begun to believe these people, and Paul was NOT happy about it! Paul spends the better part of chapters 1-5 defending the Gospel and what he taught the Galatians to help repair the damage that had been done by these intruders.

In a nutshell, these false teachers were placing a requirement for circumcision on the Galatians in order for them to be considered a Christian. Circumcision was required by Jewish law (aka the Old Testament), but under the New Covenant (aka the New Testament), Jesus' death, burial, and resurrection fulfilled the Old Testament law.

Read Galatians 3:13. Answer the questions below. HINT: the answers are in the first part of the verse before it says "for it is written..."

From what did Christ redeem us?

| |
| |

How did Christ redeem us?

| |
| |

Essentially, Paul was saying that they didn't need circumcision any longer for salvation. They now had freedom in Christ.

free in Christ

The false teachers were adding to the requirements for salvation - which is NOT the Gospel. So let's take a minute to discover what is required for salvation.

Turn to Romans 10:9-10. Write these verses below.

Circle the two requirements for salvation from the verses you wrote above. HINT: Both requirements are mentioned in verse 9 and then repeated again in verse 10.

Christ fulfilled all of the requirements for salvation. We just have to accept His free gift of salvation.

But let's not let ourselves off the hook too easily. We are often like those false teachers as we attempt to place extra requirements on ourselves and others for salvation.

We've started you off with some of those "extra requirements." Can you add to our list?

Good works.
No tattoos.
No cursing.
No drinking.
Wear dressy clothes to church.

_____

_____

_____

Disclaimer: The above list is not filled with things that are necessarily good or bad. They just should not be viewed as a requirement for salvation as some believe.

It's kind of like when our students need to pass a particular assessment. There are certain standards that they must meet in order to move on to the next level. Confessing Jesus as Lord and believing that He has risen from the dead are the only two Biblical requirements for salvation. Christ fulfilled the Old Covenant requirements through His death, burial, and resurrection.

Let's end today by listening to a song that will remind us that we can come to Jesus just as we are - no strings attached. When you're finished listening to the song, take a minute to thank the Lord for His free gift of salvation. You can write your prayer below if you'd like.

Dear Jesus,

DAY 2 — THE PROBLEM

Unfortunately, in our culture, it is a popular belief that freedom is the license to do whatever you want.

In your own words, define freedom.

[ ]

Freedom in Christ is what we defined yesterday. It is freedom from the law. It is not freedom to sin...freedom to do whatever you want...freedom to live a life without any consequences. Remember, our freedom in Christ came at a great cost - Jesus' life. Jesus in our place.

Read Galatians 5:13.

What are we NOT to do with our freedom?

[ ]

What are we to do with our freedom?

[ ]

While you're in Galatians 5, go ahead and read verses 14-15.

Verse 14 will be the focus of the remainder of our study, but before we can focus on that, we first need to focus on the problem presented in verse 15. The opposite of loving our neighbor is found in verse 15.

As a Christian, we have a war that is waging within us between the flesh and the Spirit. The flesh is the focus of verse 15. Paul further defines works of the flesh in verses 19-21. Try sorting the 15 sins of the flesh in the chart below. Some of these sins can fit into multiple categories - so no worries if you place one in multiple categories.

Sins Against Self	Sins Against Others	Sins Against God

9

Did you read verse 21? Ouch. 😲 What was your reaction when you read that verse?

Paul certainly has a way with words, doesn't he? Like the beginning of Galatians, he ain't trippin' over his words. Excuse our grammar. 😄 This verse can easily misinterpreted, misunderstood, and misused. This is what happens when people quote portions of Scripture without using the context/message of the entire Bible. God doesn't contradict Himself.

Authors David Platt and Tony Merida explain Paul's intent well:

> "...If you are living under the rule of the flesh, then you should stand in fear because you will not enter the coming kingdom. Those who came to faith in Christ by grace alone are new people (6:15). While they will still wrestle with sin, the flesh will not dominate them. They have new desires and new power to live. Our good works do not save us, but true salvation leads to fruitfulness and faithfulness."

What was Paul's point? He didn't mean that we would never sin or be tempted with sin again. He was concerned with what was ruling their lives...ours too. The problem was living and being controlled by continual and habitual sin without any desire for repentance or a plan in place to turn away from that habitual sin.

1 John 3:9 says, "No one born of God makes a practice of sinning, for God's seed abides in him; and he cannot keep on sinning, because he has been born of God."

If we are born of God, what do we not do? Underline your answer in 1 John 3:9 above.

The messages are the same both in Galatians 5:21 and 1 John 3:9. It is a matter of what you practice habitually. Ask yourself this question: what is ruling over my life - the flesh or the Spirit?

VOCABULARY TO KNOW
Repentance: to turn away from; an about face; to walk a different direction.

BAM! POW! We know this day may have smacked you in the face. You have just gone a few rounds with an ultimate fighter, Paul. Don't be discouraged; be encouraged by this verse. Find your favorite praise and worship song and spend some time coloring with Jesus.

Thanks be to God !! He gives us the VICTORY through our Lord Jesus Christ

1 Corinthians 15:57

Day 3 — The FRUited LYfe

Are you ready to ditch that **#sinlife** and live **#thefruitedlyfe**? We spent yesterday talking about sin and how habitual sin can ruin our future. Today, we begin to unpack **#thefruitedlyfe** 😎

Yes, we know that we spelled **LIFE** with a **Y**. Bethany, **#theenglishnerd** 😎, says cool middle and high schoolers spell it that way...so at the risk of being uncool, it's **#thefruitedlyfe**, y'all.

Soooo we made up a word - fruited - because we are cool like that. Well kind of...it's a REAL word. The actual word is an adjective that means "producing fruit," and while that definition works, ours is a little bit different.

FRUit + ROOted = FRUited

Let's break down each of these words.

#FRUit

Take a moment to read Galatians 5:22-23. Write down each of the nine traits of the fruit of the Spirit on the pineapple.

Did you notice that we said "fruit" not "fruits"? Paul uses the singular word here to emphasize that these character traits all work together collectively. When we have the Fruit of the Spirit, we have all of these traits working in us to make us more like Jesus.

Now, that doesn't mean that we immediately exhibit them all, but rather that the Holy Spirit works in us over time and through various circumstances in life to sharpen them and grow each one in us.

It also doesn't mean that we have to master one fruit before we move on to the next one. We have a tendency to want to focus in on one specific fruit like patience, for example. We feel that we have to master patience before we can move on to kindness. Rather than focusing on perfecting one fruit, our focus should be allowing God to mold and shape us while He produces all of His fruit in us.

We don't know about you, but patience is one fruit we fo' sho' know we have not fully mastered! It's kind of a relief knowing that we don't have to master one before moving on to another because if we did, we'd be stuck forever.

We have to stop looking at them as individual fruits and realize they are one collective Fruit. Truly, this Fruit is a description of our Savior, Jesus. He exhibits each of these character traits perfectly. It will certainly take a lifetime for us to reflect Him perfectly. In fact, we won't reflect Him perfectly until we reach Heaven. In other words, this fruit bearin' is a lifestyle. It's a lifestyle that the Holy Spirit enables us to live. And that's what we're going to see as we study each trait of the Holy Spirit's Fruit.

Look up Psalm 1:3 and write it below.

Circle the word in that verse that is a synonym for "rooted."

Underline what a rooted tree does.

On Bonnie's family's land, there is a small creek that runs through the pasture. Alongside the creek are several trees. One tree in particular was blown over during a storm. It was knocked sideways. In fact, you can still see bits of the roots growing above ground. Over the past several years, the tree has continued to live. Why? Because the roots of the tree are still connected to its life source, water.

Each spring, the tree continues to produce new leaves, and the tree flourishes from year to year. It may be leaning sideways, but the roots are strong because it is connected to the stream...just like man - or woman - mentioned in Psalm 1:3.

Without strong, healthy roots, a tree cannot produce new leaves or new fruit. A tree needs the nourishment of water to build strong roots. We can compare our lives to a tree. In order for us to produce fruit, we need strong, healthy roots.

We can't take an apple and staple it to a tree and say, "Now my tree is an apple tree!" The stapled fruit would wither and die because it would not be not connected to the root. In order for a tree to produce good fruit, it needs to be connected to the root.

Oftentimes, we try to "staple" certain fruit to our lives only to find that it doesn't work. We need a little more self control, so we try to "staple it" to our lives...not gonna work. In order for us to produce the fruit of self-control, we need to be rooted and grounded in Christ.

In order to have the fruit you've gotta have the Root

#FRUited

So what does it mean to be **#fruited**, you ask?

Being **#fruited** means that we are living a life that is rooted in Christ and His Word so that the Holy Spirit can work in us to bear the fruit, the character traits of Jesus that we see in Galatians 5:22-23.

The remainder of our study will be focused on learning how to live **#thefruitedlyfe**

Confession: we did not just spell **LIFE** with a **Y** to be cool…we are not shameless middle schoolers.

LIFE with an **I** just seems to be boring, mundane, and meaningless while **LYFE** with a **Y** has an extra spunk to it. The fruit of the Spirit helps us to stand out…just like that **Y** in **LYFE** makes the word stand out. The Fruit of the Spirit helps us to be different from the mundane world around us. It helps us to find meaning in the difficult circumstances of our personal lives and our classrooms and offers us stability and a different perspective. The fruit simply gives us **#lyfe**

So who's ready to live…

#THEFRUITEDLYFE

DAY 4 — LEMONY SWEET

In order for us to live **#thefruitedlyfe,** we need to understand three sections into which the Fruit of the Spirit are divided. Raise your hand if you already knew that the Fruit of the Spirit was divided into three sections. 'Cause we fo' sho' didn't know before we began this journey 😊 so we are guessing several of you are probably in the same boat as us.

What are those sections, you ask?

Our relationship with God.

Our relationship with others.

Our relationship with ourselves.

Every good teacher doesn't just GIVE you the answers, and we claim to be good teachers! So, we must make you figure out which fruit goes with which section.

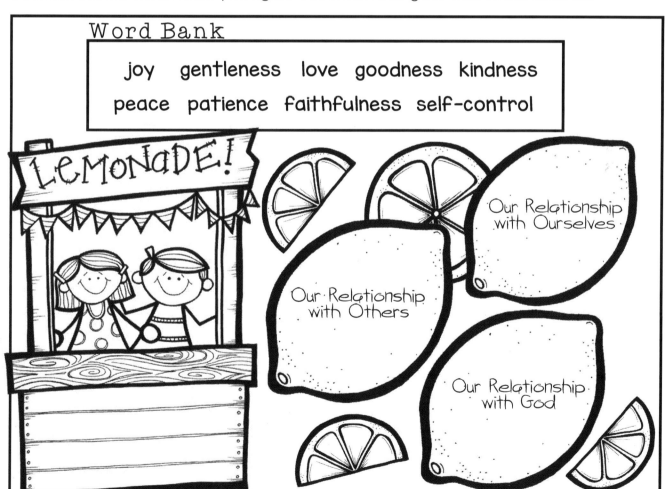

Word Bank

joy   gentleness   love   goodness   kindness
peace   patience   faithfulness   self-control

LEMONADE!

Our Relationship with Others

Our Relationship with Ourselves

Our Relationship with God

DAY 4 — LEMONY SWEET

How'd you do? Easy peasy lemon squeezy? Or did that leave a sour taste of confusion in your mouth?

Well, the answer is probably a tad more simplistic than you might think at first glance. Paul so kindly listed them in order for us. And for perfectionistic peeps like us, they fit nice and evenly into these three sections...three in each. Let's take a look.

The ANSWER KEY

joy   gentleness   love   goodness   kindness
peace   patience   faithfulness   self-control

LEMONADE!

faithfulness
Our Relationship with Ourselves
self-control
gentleness

kindness
Our Relationship with Others
patience
goodness

Our Relationship with God
joy   love
peace

Many Bible scholars believe and agree that the Fruit can be divided into these three sections. While each part of the fruit can certainly stand alone, we can see how the three in each category work together to strengthen each respective relationship - with God, others, or ourselves. As we study the Fruit of the Spirit and learn to live this **#fruitedlyfe**, we will understand how the lemony-goodness of each can be squeezed together to make the perfect glass of lemonade - not too sweet, not too tart, but justtttttt right. Goldilocks perfection! 😊

17

DAY 4 — LEMONY SWEET

As we end our first week together, let's spend some time in prayer asking the Lord to prepare us for what's ahead as He helps us grow in our relationship with Him and with others. We want to come out lemony sweet, not bitter and tart.

Dear Jesus,

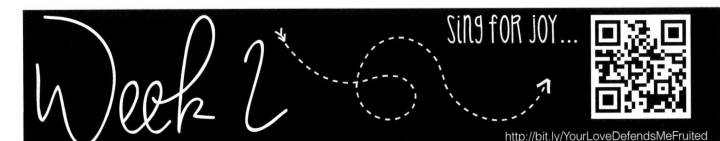

SCRIPTURE MEMORY: "Blessed is the man who trusts in the LORD, whose trust is the LORD. He is like a tree planted by water, that sends out its roots by the stream, and does not fear when heat comes, for its leaves remain green, and is not anxious in the year of drought, for it does not cease to bear fruit." Jeremiah 17:7-8

Have you ever had a student in your classroom teach you something about God's goodness and His love? I love teaching kindergarten because it has taught me, Bonnie, more about what Jesus meant when He said that we are to have childlike faith. Kindergarteners generally love quickly, trust wholeheartedly, and rejoice unashamedly in small moments.

I have a kindergarten student this year that requires a little extra love from me, his teacher. While that is true, he himself is quick to love me, too. In fact, the first time I met this little guy, he told me that he loved me and that I was beautiful. In that moment, he had no clue what the days ahead would look like as our teacher/student relationship was just beginning to take root. He just loved, and in that same moment, I fell in love with his zeal for life.

Just before every break, I take a moment to hug each of my students, kiss the tops of their heads, and look into their eyes as I say, "I love you. Have a good break!" As we prepared to leave for spring break, my little friend hugged me tightly and told me that he would miss me. On the day we returned from spring break, I stood at my door greeting each of my students. One or two students grinned as they walked past me, filing into the door of my classroom. A few more students hugged me as they reached my doorway. I caught a glimpse of still more students grinning from ear to ear as they rounded the corner and saw me at the door, but the moment my special friend rounded the corner and could see me standing there, his arms went up into the air for a hug as he began to run full force toward me. It didn't matter that big kids were barriers at that moment, blocking his way to my arms. He ran, shouting along the way at the top of his lungs, "I MISSED YOU!!!! I LOVE YOU SO MUCH! OH! I MISSED YOU! DID YOU KNOW THAT I LOVE YOU!?!?" 😎 The moment he reached me, he jumped into my arms, not another care in the world because all was right in his little kindergartener world. Such life. Such love.

Our walk with Jesus is just like my little friend. Past days didn't matter to him. Mistakes from earlier days didn't matter to him. All that mattered is that we were back together.

I don't know where you are in your walk with the Lord in this moment. Maybe you have felt some distance between you and God or maybe your walk is closer than it has ever been. Wherever you are in your walk with Jesus, He is standing there waiting for you to run and jump into His arms, so everything will be right again because you're back together. God is the one that is saying, "I missed you! I love you so much! Oh! I missed you! Did you know that I love you?!"

Sweet teacher friends, be like my little kinder baby and run whole-heartedly towards the open arms of Jesus and experience His never-ending love. Oh how He loves us!

love (agapē) noun
1. One of Paul's most frequently used words
2. occurs 75 times in the New Testament
3. occurs 34 times in Paul's writings

Fill in the blank.

"But the fruit of the Spirit is _____, joy, peace, patience, kindness, goodness, faithfulness, gentleness, and self control."
Galatians 5:22

We, Bonnie and Bethany, LOVE coffee. We LOVE flair pens. We LOVE the Dollar Tree and the dollar section of Target. We cannot deny our LOVE of food. We LOVE to get our nails done. 😎

Yes, we know that these are all really superficial things. List some of the superficial things that you LOVE.

We *also* LOVE God's Word. We LOVE our family. We LOVE our students. We LOVE our church. We LOVE our friendships. 😎

These are not as superficial. List some things you love that are more significant than your first list.

We tend to throw around the word LOVE for a variety of different things that we have affection for in our lives. Love is one of those words that is complex...kind of like an onion. It has many layers and shades of meaning. When we say that we LOVE flair pens, it does not equal to the same kind of LOVE we have for God's Word.

While this is an issue for us, this was not the case in Jesus' time. They had many different words to express different types of love. In order to understand the word LOVE in Galatians 5, let's look at a conversation Jesus had about LOVE.

Read Mark 12:28-34.

What question is asked of Jesus in verse 28?

Fill in the blanks below from Mark 12:29-31.

"Jesus answered, 'The most important is, 'Hear, O Israel: The Lord our God, the Lord is one. And you shall _____ the Lord your God with all your heart and with all your soul and with all your mind and with all your strength.' The second is this: 'You shall _____ your neighbor as yourself.' There is no other commandment greater than these."

Jesus is quoting Deuteronomy 6:4-5 and Leviticus 19:18b.

The scribe asked Jesus what the most important commandment was, and He responded with TWO commandments instead of one. Why do you think he did that?

Well, to Jesus, these are seen as one commandment; they are equal. When you love God, you love people. When you love people, it is because you love God.

In kindergarten math, we discuss flipping addends. In the equation 2 + 3 = 5, both 2 and 3 are considered addends.

2 + 3 = 5   3 + 2 = 5   5 = 2 + 3   5 = 3 + 2   5 = 5

No matter how you write it or flip it, when the numbers 2 and 3 are added together, it will always equal 5. Loving God = Loving People. The reverse is true as well: Loving People = Loving God.

DAY 1 NO GREATER LOVE

http://bit.ly/NoGreaterLoveFruited

The meaning behind the LOVE that Jesus was talking about is certainly different than the type of LOVE we were referencing on our superficial list. The LOVE for our flair pens isn't the same kind of LOVE that He intended for us to have for Him. Not by a long shot!

Remember that LOVE is a word with many shades of meaning. The LOVE a mother has for her son is far different from the LOVE a husband has for his wife.

The LOVE that Jesus was commanding us to have for Him and for our neighbors is called agapē love. It is a sacrificial love. It is a selfless love. It is the same love that God demonstrated to us when He sent His one and only Son to die on the cross for us. Jesus also demonstrated this type of love when He willingly gave up His life for us - for sinners - on the cross.

This love, this agapē love, is the type of LOVE that Paul is talking about in Galatians 5. He is exhorting us to demonstrate this kind of sacrifice, this kind of selflessness.

We want to end today by having you listen to one of our favorite songs...from circa 2002. We vividly recall our 16 and 17 year old selves driving around, listening to our friend, Rachel Lampa, belt out "No Greater Love." We may or may not have joined her in said belting. Bonnie's 1996 Chevy Cavalier's speaker was busted and would only play at the volume of extremely loud. She didn't mind. The louder it was, the more she loved Jesus. Bethany's purple Hyundai Elantra had no speaker issues, but she cranked the volume because that's the only way to listen to Rachel Lampa's hit song. Again...the louder it is, the more you love Jesus, right? So whether or not you enjoyed Rachel Lampa back in the day, join our little throwback and belt out a note or two with us...or just sit and enjoy hearing the simple truth of the gospel from a powerful song artist.

22

We ended yesterday by having you to listen to the song "No Greater Love" by Rachael Lampa. To us, this song is a great presentation of the gospel. There is *no* greater example of agapē love. A love so great demands a response.

Yesterday, we briefly mentioned Deuteronomy 6:4-5. Go ahead and flip to that passage and read it.

Fill in the blanks.

"You shall love the LORD your God with **all** your _____ and with **all**

your _____ and with **all** your _____."

Deuteronomy 6:4-5 should be our response to what Jesus did for us.

LOVING GOD WITH ALL YOUR HEART

In order for us to understand how to love God with all our heart, we must know what the Bible says about our hearts. Proverbs 4:23 is a great place to begin. Take a look:

"Guard your heart above all else, for it is the source of life." (CSB)

"Keep your heart with all vigilance, for from it flow the springs of life." (ESV)

"Watch over your heart with all diligence, for from it flow the springs life." (NASB)

"Above all else, guard your heart, for everything you do flows from it." (NIV)

Essentially, this verse - no matter the version - is saying that whatever is inside our hearts will flow out into our lives and pour out to those around us. Our heart influences everything we do. This is true physically and spiritually. Physically, if our heart stops beating, we are dead. Spiritually, if our hearts are filled with hatred, bitterness, and sin, we are dead inside.

Jump back to the Proverbs 4:23...the very reason God wants us to guard our hearts is because life springs from what is in our hearts, so we must filter what we allow in our hearts.

Our desires flow from our heart.
Our thoughts flow from our heart.
Our attitudes flow from our heart.
Our outlook flows from our heart.

https://www.desiringgod.org/articles/love-god-with-your-everything

In the hearts below, write examples of things we should allow into our hearts and things from which we should guard our hearts.

Allow in our hearts...

Guard our hearts from...

LOVING GOD WITH ALL YOUR SOUL

When you fly on a plane, the number of living bodies on the plane is described as souls. There are three separate numbers that are used to calculate this number of souls: the number of passengers, the number of crew members, and the number of babies on laps. All of those numbers added together are considered to be souls.

Biblically speaking, Genesis 2:7 provides us with the definition of a soul: "And the LORD God formed man of the dust of the ground, and breathed into his nostrils the breath of life; and man became a **living soul**." (KJV)

God's breath in us makes us a living soul. Our soul is an extension of our heart. A living person's soul includes the heart yet is so much more. Our soul is what we say and how we react to situations in our lives. Our soul is the outward action that stems from our desires, thoughts, attitudes, and outlook.

Everything about us should declare that God is supreme. Our speech, talents, and reactions should reflect our love for God. People should know we are His simply by watching us and listening to us. Who we are should scream, "We are His!"

"As in water face reflects face, so the heart of man reflects the man." Proverbs 27:19

We don't know about you, but we just said, "Ouch!" 😮

24

https://www.desiringgod.org/articles/love-god-with-your-everything

I, Bonnie, have foot-in-mouth disease. 😜 More times than not, my speech gets the best of me. My parents raised me to be a strong, bold, independent woman. My boldness sometimes comes out in my speech. Over the years, I have had to learn to respond rather than react to situations. I consistently pray over the words that I use on a daily basis.

While we normally ask you to pray at the end of a day's study, today, we feel like you should take a moment and ask God to help your speech, talents, and reactions to reflect your love for Him. Ask Him to help you love Him with all your soul.

LOVING GOD WITH ALL YOUR MIGHT

Okay, where are all the **#englishnerds** 🤓? Something pretty interesting is happening in this portion of the text. The word might/strength is normally used as the adverb "very." However, in this case it is used as a noun. This happens in only ONE other place in the Old Testament.

Look up and read 2 Kings 23:25.

Sound familiar? This verse is basically repeating the Deuteronomy 6:5 passage.

So, what exactly does this mean? We should love the Lord our God with all of our heart, with all of our soul, and all of our *very*? Excuse our southern, but that doesn't make a lick of sense. Remember, in this case, the word is being used as a noun. When it is translated as a noun, it means "abundance."

Let's concentrate on the word **abundance.**

Normally, when we think of the words might/strength, we think about power and physical strength. This verse seems to be describing so much more than physical power. Just like loving God with all of our soul is an extension of loving God with all of our heart, loving God with all of our strength/might is an extension of loving Him with all of our soul. When we love Him in our abundance, we are loving Him with all of the resources we have been given.

We love Him with the tools He has given to us. Every resource that we have around is used to point to Him. That means the computer I use should be used to glorify God. It also means the home I am living in should be used to glorify Him. As a teacher, it means the resources that God has given me, should be used to glorify my Heavenly Father.

We use our **abundance** to point to Him.

It does not matter if your "abundance" is little or much, it is all of His, all of the time, all for His glory.

25

DAY 2 LOVING GOD

OUR RESPONSE

What should be our response to the information we just learned?

Flip back a couple of pages to the beginning of this day. The first task we gave you was to fill in the blanks for Deuteronomy 6:5. What word did we mark in **bold** letters? Write it big and bold below.

The reminder that we should love God with **ALL** our heart, **ALL** our soul, and **ALL** our might, means that our desires/affections should never be divided.

We can't act one way in our intimate moments of worshiping God and act a completely different way when are standing before our students in the classroom.

Loving God means that it influences our whole life: our thoughts, words, and behavior.
Loving God means that we honor Him in our giving.
Loving God means that we honor Him in our time.
Loving God means that we have no room for any other affection.

Loving God means ______________________________

Loving God means______________________________

"THE BIBLE CALLS US TO *wholehearted, life-encompassing,* COMMUNITY-IMPACTING, *exclusive commitment* TO OUR GOD." -Jason DeRouchie

https://www.desiringgod.org/articles/love-god-with-your-everything

Loving God is possibly the easier of these two commands. Loving people...welllllll that's another story.

Let's go back to Mark 12. Turn there and read verses 29-31.

Write verse 31a below.

Jesus' two greatest commandments both find their root in the fruit of love. We've spent the last two days looking at the command: love the Lord your God with all your heart, soul, and might. Today, we're going to tackle this often difficult task of loving people.

First of all, perhaps we should point out that Jesus told us to love our neighbors as ourselves. We love ourselves waaaaaay more than we care to admit. In fact, our culture is a self-love culture. We are all about promoting self-love...sometimes even at the expense of loving others. **#yikes**

We love ourselves when...

...we feed ourselves meals and snacks.
...we buy things for ourselves.
...we focus on our life and the things that are going on in our personal world.

So when He commands us to love others as we love ourselves, He's talking about being givers and taking our self-focus and making it others-focused.

It is easier to love certain people. Lovable people are easy to love. That's most likely not who Jesus was referring to with this command since loving lovable people is easy. His focus was most likely on loving the unloveable. Sooo...how exactly do we go about that, you may ask? Before we answer that...

What are some things in a person that would make you say they were unloveable?

DaY 3   LoViNg PeoPLe

To us, someone that is unloveable is... 😖 😲 🙄 😠 ☹️

...the kid who always cops an attitude.
...the parent who continually puts us down or undermines us.
...the administrator who doesn't know our value.
...the coworker who disapproves of the way that we teach.
...the outsider who believes that teachers are just glorified babysitters.

So now that we have an idea of what unloveable looks like, let's go back to the question: how do we go about loving unloveable people?

Well, first and foremost, we must recognize that our love for people flows out of our love for God. As we practice loving God with all of our heart, soul, mind, and strength, loving our neighbors - whether they're lovely or unloveable - becomes easier and, dare we say it, more natural.

The best way to understand this command is to figure out what this looks like practically in our lives and in our classrooms.

In our personal lives and/or classrooms, what are some practical ways we can love unloveable people?

In moments where we are loving the unloveable, we have never been more like Jesus. He is King of loving unloveable people. After all, let's be real: WE are the unloveable. We are sinners. We are rotten and **#rottenfruitaintgood** There is absolutely not a single reason in the world that He should have loved us, yet He did...just because.

When we are around the unloveable, do they feel Jesus' love? Do they see Him in us? Or do we allow them to feel our distance as we focus more on self than others? Do they sense our disdain of them?

Our prayer for you and for ourselves is that we ooze Jesus. We want people to sense Him in us and hear Him as we speak. We want people - lovely people *and* unloveable people - to see Jesus in us.

As you listen to the song linked below and color, prayerfully consider the questions our friend, Joy Williams, is asking herself and us.

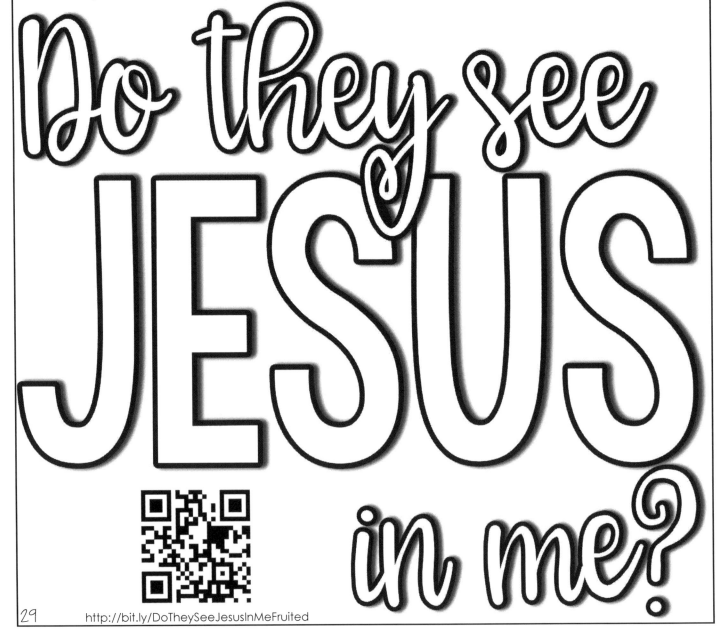

Do they see JESUS in me?

http://bit.ly/DoTheySeeJesusInMeFruited

Day 4 It's Rainin' Love

Have you ever been stuck somewhere without an umbrella when lo and behold the most massive storm pops up just when you need to leave? This happened to me, Bethany, not so long ago. I was at Bonnie's house when the rain came a-pourin'! Where were my umbrellas, you ask? Not in my purse. Not in my teacher bag. Not anywhere helpful. They were in...yep...you guessed it - my car. 😐 Sheesh. I was about to get drenched...and I don't know about you, but I hate getting soaked. It's like the wet goes through you and then you're shivering and miserable. Bleh. Thankfully, right before I stepped outside, Bonnie came to my rescue. She found an umbrella! I popped that thing up and walked to my car protected from the craziness pouring down around me.

Isn't life sometimes like that? It's like the world just starts pouring down its negativity, its harshness, its condemnation. Yuck. The last thing we want is to be drenched in such "rain." When we're caught out in the middle of these worldly storms without our umbrella, we're just out of luck. It's like the negativity and harshness and condemnation just seeps into our very core. Not a good look on us. 😬

Love is our umbrella. You see, underneath the umbrella of love, not only do we find protection from the world's massive storms of ickiness, but we also find all the other Fruit of the Spirit. The other 8 characteristics stem from this love we've talked about this week.

Without love, we won't have joy. Without love, we won't have peace. Without love, we definitely won't have patience. Without love, kindness, goodness, faithfulness, and gentleness wouldn't be a thing in our lives. They all - every Fruit of the Spirit - begin with love. 😘

And let us not forget, this love train all began when God the Father made the incredibly humbling plan to send His Son to die for us, sinners...so underserving. That, dear friends, is love.

30

When we pop up the umbrella of love, **we stand out**. We find that while others around us are drenched with negativity, harshness, condemning spirits, we are wrapped in the cloak of God's love, which, in turn, allows us to love those around us with His love.

When we pop up the umbrella of love, **we guard our hearts**. We are allowing the Holy Spirit to keep out what isn't of Him and keep in what is of Him. The more of Him that He can pour in, the more of Him we have to pour out.

When we pop up the umbrella of love, **we have an umbrella to share** with the people walking beside us. We can invite them to come under our umbrella of love as we share with them the love of our Savior.

http://bit.ly/ShelterFruited

As we begin to walk through the remainder of the Fruit of the Spirit, keep in mind that every single one of them stems from love - God's love.

God's love is **a stand out kind of love**. It's a love that we don't deserve, yet He insists on giving it to us day in and day out.

God's love is **a shelter for us**; it is our guard. When things around us get stormy and just plain crazy, we can run to the shelter of His love and find peace and safety and security as He is our anchor in the midst of the worst storms.

God's love is **a multiplying kind of love**. When we get under His umbrella of love, we can't help but pour it right back out to those around us.

On the next page, you will find an empty box. As you listen to the song below and reflect on God's love, turn to 1 Corinthians 13:4-8 and write Paul's description of love. You can make it as fancy schmancy as you'd like or as plain Jane as you'd like. 😊 We'd LOVE to see your creations on Instagram or Facebook using the hashtag **#fruited**.

DAY 4   It's Rainin' Love

1 Corinthians 13:4-8

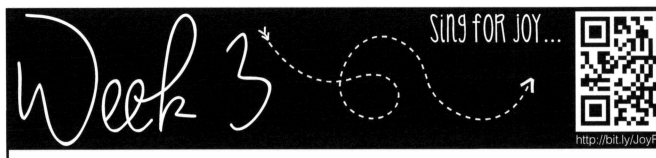
SCRIPTURE MEMORY: "Strive for peace with everyone, and for the holiness without which no one will see the Lord." Hebrews 12:14

It doesn't take much to make a kindergartener joyful.

Give them Dojo points, they're joyful.
Let them move their Sit Spots to a place they choose, they're joyful...like *really* joyful!
Take them outside, they're joyful.
Let them be the line leader for the day, they're joyful.

Joy isn't hard to come by when you're in a 5-year old little body.

Middle and high school students are surprisingly easy to make joyful, too.

Give seniors scratch 'n sniff stickers, they're joyful.
Make cake pops for them...or any food, honestly, they're joyful.
Give them "Drop Your Lowest Quiz Grade" coupons, they're joyful.
Hand them a package of M&M's for a connotation/denotation lesson, they're joyful.

Joy isn't too awfully hard to come by when you're in a middle or high school body.

These kinds of joy are short-lived. It doesn't matter if you're 5 or 12 or 18, joys like these can easily be dashed.

The Dojo points can be subtracted when Sammy decides to push his friend.
The Sit Spots might go right back to where they were when your friend can't keep her hands to herself.
Outside time does have to come to an end.
Their time as the line leader has to change because everyone can't be the leader everyday.

Scratch 'n sniff stickers eventually lose their smell.
Food gets eaten and disappears.
The "Drop Your Lowest Quiz Grade" coupon can only help once.
The M&M's will be gone in a matter of minutes.

These kinds of joy fade.

So...the question is: is this really joy? Is this quick fading characteristic of life what Paul was talking about in Galatians 5:22? That is exactly what we are going to find out as we study this week.

Grab your Bible, your favorite pen, and your favorite drink, and let's learn how to have the "joy, joy, joy, joy, down in [our] heart[s]..."

joy (chará)
noun

1. cheerfulness, calm delight, gladness, greatly exceeding joy
2. occurs 59 times

Fill in the blank.

"But the fruit of the Spirit is love,

_____ , peace, patience, kindness, goodness, faithfulness, gentleness, and self control."
Galatians 5:22

Psalm 30:5b tells us that "[w]eeping may stay overnight, but there is JOY in the morning."

Maybe it is just us, but sometimes when we read the above verse, we think, *Let me hurry up and go to sleep, so this sorrow that I feel will turn into joy.* Instead, what happens when we wake up is that we find our hearts aching just as much as the night before. It's like the nightmare that never ends. ☹

Can you relate? Think of a time in your life where you may have had a hard time finding joy in difficult circumstances.

DAY 1 JOY in SUFFERING

As humans, we sometimes believe the lie that joy is only found in the peaceful and easy moments of our lives. Joy is **not** a moment of fleeting happiness, however, but instead is lasting and sustaining. In order to obtain a joy-filled life, we must first understand where our joy is found.

Paul would be the first one to testify that joy is not always found in moments where everything in life is good and pleasant.

Look up and read Philippians 3:1 and 4:4 where Paul writes from prison. Write Philippians 4:4 below.

The source of joy is not found in the circumstances of our lives but is found in the One who gives joy. In John 17:6-19, Jesus prays for His disciples before His death on the Cross. Read that passage then write below what Jesus prays for His disciples to have in verse 13.

The source of joy is found in Jesus. Our joy is made complete in His death, burial, and resurrection (1 John 1:4). We have joy through our relationship to God through Christ. Jesus removed despair and despondency for joy and peace on the Cross.

We interrupt our regularly scheduled Bible study for a quick VOCABULARY lesson.

In this study, we have encouraged you to have strong roots so that it will show in the fruit you produce. In order to have a greater understanding of JOY, we must go back to the ROOT of the word, chará (joy). The root word for joy (char-) is also the same root word for the Greek word for grace (charis). The words joy and grace are closely connected. Joy is found through the grace of the cross.

Look up and read Hebrews 12:1-2.

Our joy comes from the victory found in Jesus' death, burial, and resurrection. The "joy that was set before Him" was satisfying the wrath of God toward us through His death on the Cross. Jesus died in our place and that brings us joy. Looking back to Philippians 4:4, Paul writes for us to rejoice in the Lord always! Paul is reminding us that our joy begins with remembering the Cross. We are grossly mistaken when we believe that joy can be found in anything but celebrating what Jesus did for us on the cross. Once we rejoice in the Cross, we will obtain true, lasting joy in the midst of life's circumstances. Joy does not come from our circumstances, but rather joy comes in rejoicing in the Cross of Christ.

Once we begin to view life through the lens of the Cross, we will be able to find and focus on joy. If our focus is on Christ, the circumstances of our lives will be viewed through the filter of the joy that is in Christ.

Around the edges of the sunglasses, write circumstances in your life that have been or are currently difficult. On the lenses of the glasses, you will see Scripture verses that refer to joy that is found in Christ. Choose one or two passages and write them on the lines of the sunglasses.

Psalm 32:11
Psalm 51:8
Psalm 51:12
Psalm 63:7

Psalm 71:23
Habakkuk 3:18
John 16:24
Romans 15:13

God has not promised us a life that is free from pain and heartache. In fact, we would venture to say that the Christian life is full of hurt, heartache, and sorrow. God DOES promise us, however, that He will walk with us through life's storms.

Open your Bible and read Matthew 14:22-33. Look at verses 29 and 30. What happens when Peter starts to focus on the strength of the storm?

When we focus on the storms of our lives, we begin to sink. This storm was not a surprise to Jesus. Jesus had a purpose in sending His disciples into the storm. He wanted to teach them how to deepen their faith and test what faith they already had. The storms we face are not a surprise to Jesus. Though this may be a tough pill to swallow, there is purpose in our storms. We may not ever understand why we face certain storms, but undoubtedly, God chooses to mold us to become more like Him in the midst of chaotic life storms. We are to "run the race that is set before us, keeping our eyes on Jesus…"

Jesus is our Anchor. He is our Deliverer. He never falters.

Let Christy Knockels sing those words over you today as you reflect on how to find joy in suffering.

There are many distractions that can happen in a classroom. It may be the kid in the back of the room that is spinning in circles instead of completing the assigned center or maybe the kid that finds it necessary to endlessly tap the end of a pencil on a desk. Whether it is the annoying tap of a pencil or the gymnastics session happening in the back of your classroom, these distractions usually take our focus off what is important and cause us to focus on the distraction. As teachers, we know that we must fix those distractions in order to promote an environment of learning. In life, we face distractions that, for a time, may alter our focus and ultimately end up stealing our joy if we aren't careful.

Distractions can be defined as anything that causes us to take our eyes off of Jesus. Distractions are joy stealers.

Yesterday, we read Hebrews 12:1-2. Go ahead and read that passage again.

Hebrews 12:1-2 reminds us to lay aside every hindrance and sin that so easily ensnares us and run the race that is set before us. Take a moment to write things in the box that may distract you from your race with Jesus. Remember, this is anything that distracts you from focusing on Jesus. On the cute little runner, write Hebrews 12:1-2.

Most distractions fall into three categories: **comparison**, **self-centeredness**, and **pride**. These distractions often lead to a faulty focus. When our focus is off, we begin to lose the joy that is found in Christ.

THE DISTRACTION OF COMPARISON

- If I only had a cute classroom like my neighbor teacher...
- Ugh! She only has 15 students, and I have 30 students.
- Sure, she can be a great teacher...she has a ton of resources, and I have to buy everything with money from my own pocket!
- Why does she get great kids while I have a classroom full of major needs?
- I could enjoy teaching so much more if I had a husband that made a ton of money like the teacher down the hall.
- Yeah, I could do all those fun things in my classroom if I were single. Single teachers have ALL the time in the world.
- God has given her all the creativity...if I just had an ounce of her creativity.

Nothing can rob you of your joy quicker than comparing your life circumstances to someone else's. Running coaches tell runners to keep their eyes focused on the finish line. If a runner is busy looking at his or her competitor, then it will slow the runner's pace. It is not our job to worry about someone else's race. We must stay in our lane and run the race the God has set before us.

Have you struggled with the distraction of comparison? List things from your life that you often compare to the lives of others.

THE DISTRACTION OF SELF-CENTEREDNESS

Once we start comparing our lives to someone else's life, it can easily turn our focus to self. We quickly become consumed with ourselves in the midst of our comparison. Self-centeredness turns into self-absorption and self-pity.

- Why didn't my neighbor teacher say hello to me today?
- Why didn't my administrator offer to help me when he saw me moving boxes?
- I've been out for two days. Isn't anyone going to call or text me to check on me?
- I need an aide. I know I have just as many kids as the third grade teacher, but I need an aide, and I need one now!

Take one of the distractions of comparison that you listed on the previous page and discuss how that comparison could turn into self-centeredness.

[ ]

THE DISTRACTION OF PRIDE

Self-centeredness can easily turn into pride. It crosses that line when I demand that you do things my way because I am right, and you are obviously oh-so-wrong.

Focusing on self eventually becomes a form of pride when we feel like...
- ...our way is the best.
- ...we find satisfaction in our own achievements without considering who helped us accomplish those achievements.
- ...our needs are more important than others' needs.

Ultimately, it becomes a vicious cycle of comparison that leads to self-centeredness that turns into pride. If we are not careful, the cycle repeats itself over and over, stealing our joy that is found in Christ.

When I, Bonnie, was in college, I had a roommate who would often disagree with me on how to handle household chores and cooking responsibilities. It sounds so trivial...and quite frankly, our arguments were trivial. We were both raised differently. We were both taught to cook in different ways. We were both VERY strong willed, and our own personal way was the RIGHT way. Our strong wills - aka PRIDE - got us into many disagreements about how to handle cleaning and which way was the best way to boil chicken. Instead of learning from one another, we allowed pride to enter into our roommate relationship.

Can you think of an example where your pride may rear its ugly head at school? What about in your life?

[ ]

SIDE NOTE

Okay, remember when we said that most distractions from joy could fit into those nice three little categories? Key Word MOST.

We found one distraction that we felt could easily steal your joy, but unfortunately, no matter how hard we tried, it did not fit into those categories, but it was too important for us to leave out of the study.

So here is a bonus distraction...if we can even count it a bonus?!

DISTRACTION OF LOOKING TO THE FUTURE

Future planning is not always a bad thing. In fact, we both tend to be planners. Planning what is going to happen in the future is in our nature. As teachers, we map out our weeks and months to fill the school year. We may plan for a future vacation. We may map out our financial future. Future planning isn't necessarily a bad thing.

However, we find ourselves in trouble when we are LIVING in a constant state of the future. Have you ever had any of these thoughts?

- **The Countdowns:**
  - There are 10 more days until our next break!
  - We have 5 more Mondays until the end of the school year!
  - 174 days until these students graduate!

- **The "Just One More's:"**
  - Just one more year in this grade level and then maybe I can move to the grade I want.
  - Just one more month, and I will be finished with this grad school class.
  - Just one more year in this district then I can move schools.

- **The "I Can't Wait's:"**
  - I can't wait until I have a new class next year.
  - I can't wait until I get married.
  - I can't wait until I have a baby.
  - I can't wait until my baby is out of diapers.
  - I can't wait until this sports season ends.
  - I can't wait until Christmas is over.
  - I can't wait until warm summer months.

We get so busy looking at what may or may not lie ahead in our future that we forget the present race we are running. We live our lives in the future and never find contentment in the present.

> "Wherever you are, be all there! Live to the hilt every situation you believe to be the will of God." -Jim Elliot

No matter what our present circumstances look like, God has something for us to learn in the right now. If we continue to focus on our future and ignore the present, it will rob us of our joy, and we will end up wasting our lives always focused on the next thing.

FINISHING THE RACE WELL

So how do we finish the race well? How do we train ourselves to focus more on the present rather than always looking ahead to the future? On our cute, little runner, write practical action steps you can take that will help you from becoming distracted.

Fill in the blank.

"But the fruit of the Spirit is love, joy _____, patience, kindness, goodness, faithfulness, gentleness, and self control."
Galatians 5:22

Raise your hand if you love cute kids! We're raising both hands! Bonus points for a cute kid who can sing! If you haven't already, you're going to want to go watch our sweet, cute, little girl sing. The link is below. We'll meet you back here when you're finished dabbing your eyes dry...because there's just something about a little baby singing about Jesus that makes you wanna cry.

peace (eirēnē)
noun
1. peace between individuals, i.e. harmony, concord
2. security, safety, prosperity, felicity, (because peace and harmony make and keep things safe and prosperous)
3. the tranquil state of a soul assured of its salvation...fearing nothing from God and content...
4. occurs 92 times

http://bit.ly/PeaceInChristFruited

Isn't she adorable?? We love her! And we love the message of the song she is singing. Peace seems to be absent from our world today, doesn't it? The promise of her words rings true: "When there's no peace on earth, there is peace in Christ."

The next two days, we want to explore what Biblical peace really is.

We have given you the New Testament definition for eirēnē, which is the Greek word for peace, but how would you define peace?

[text box]

Most people believe that the word peace means "the absence of war." However, the Bible has a slightly different definition. To help us understand the Biblical meaning behind the word peace, we need to understand how it is used in the Hebrew (The Old Testament) and the Greek (The New Testament).

Shalom (Hebrew)

In the Old Testament, peace **can** mean the absence of conflict, but often, it points us to the presence of something better in its place. The word shalom basically means wholeness or completeness. Shalom is something that is multi-faceted and complex with many parts that come together and work as a whole…kind of like a puzzle. Peace is not *just* war ending. Peace is a coming together of both sides to work together and flourish in the aftermath of war.

Think about a teacher that you struggled to get along with at some point. Maybe you disagreed on a methodology of teaching a particular topic. Or maybe one teacher does room transformations and her partner teacher doesn't, and she's made to feel inadequate because that's just not her style of teaching. Peace is not just cohabitating in this situation; peace is coming together and working together and learning to appreciate the other person's teaching style while learning from them.

Can you think of a situation in your workplace when things were not peaceful? What were the circumstances like during this time?

[text box]

If you're presently in a situation like that - one that lacks peace - what are some practical ways you can bring peace in the midst of that war?

Let's be **#englishnerds** 😎 for a minute. When we change the part of speech for a word, it sometimes changes the definition. Let's take the word *table* as an example. When used as a noun, a table is a place to sit and eat or a place to set items for display, etc. (Example: Please set the table for dinner.) When table is used as a verb, it means to postpone something indefinitely. (Example: Since we can't agree on this issue, let's just table it and move on for now.)

Hebrew is no different. So let's see how the Hebrew word for peace, shalom, is defined when used as a noun and then as a verb.

Shalom as a noun.
Shalom is a state of being or wellness. Shalom was used as a common greeting, essentially, to wish a blessing of health and prosperity with mind, soul, and body.
We confess that often we struggle with fear and fight the battle for peace in our mind quite frequently. If you're like us, when we get a parent email that expresses frustration that doesn't place blame on the child, but rather on us, we lack peace...like to the point of not being able to sleep or focus on much of anything else. 😟 Even when teaching, we find ourselves distracted, thinking about that email and replaying its words over and over and over again. If we were at a place of shalom, we would not have sleepless nights and restless days.

Have you ever been there?

DAY 3   PEACE IN CHRIST

Shalom as a verb.
To bring shalom would be to restore something that has been lost or broken or to finish something that is incomplete.

Let's look at a few examples:

 As teachers, we often spend our days solving drama and conflicts that may arise. We are technically bringing shalom as we reconcile relationships.

 Sometimes it's hard to come together as teachers to meet about something because one of our team members is always missing. We find shalom when everyone is present again.

 In kindergarten, when little Johnny loses a shoe, shalom is missing until the shoe is found.

 In middle school, when Henry can't find his homework in his dumpster-like book bag, shalom is missing until he cleans it out and finds his homework paper crumpled up at the bottom of the bag.

 In high school, when Mikey's tablet is not working properly for the millionth time, shalom is missing until the IT person can fix it.

In the Old Testament, the Israelites were in search of shalom. They felt like shalom would be brought upon them in the form of an earthly king, yet, it wasn't. In fact, many of their kings proved to be ungodly and were antagonistic toward peace.

In order to discover what - or rather Who - brought peace to the Israelites, we need to move from the Hebrew word, shalom, to the Greek word, eirēnē. What was started in the Old Testament was fulfilled in the New Testament. We will dive right in tomorrow.

In the meantime, spend some time in prayer, asking God to show you ways that you can promote peace in your relationships.

Not long ago, in Bonnie's kindergarten classroom, her students were completing puzzles. One little friend decided that he wanted to be the one who put in the last puzzle piece, so he hid a piece in the classroom, so his friends could not find it. When all but the last piece was together, he announced to his friends, "I hid it! **#stinker** Because I wanted to be the person to put in the last piece of the puzzle!" The opposite of peace ensued as his friends became very angry that the missing puzzle piece was hidden somewhere in the classroom. To bring **peace**, they had to find the missing **piece**.

The Israelites were missing a **piece** of their **peace** as well. They believed that their missing **piece** was a king, but the missing **piece** wasn't found until Jesus' birth.

Eirēnē (Greek)

The Old Testament search for shalom was answered in the New Testament coming of Jesus. Jesus became the Israelites' Eirēnē. He was their **Peace**. He was their *missing* **piece**. He is our missing **piece** as well.

Look up Romans 5:1 and write it below.

```



```

Without Jesus, our relationship with God is broken. Through Jesus, our relationship with God has been restored to wholeness. Jesus is our Eirēnē. Jesus is our **Peace**. Jesus is our missing **piece**.

Look up Romans 14:19 and write it below.

```



```

As Christians, because we have the peace of Christ within us, we are called to spread that peace to one another. Our role as a believer, our goal is to do whatever it takes to promote peace within our homes, our workplaces, our relationships, our churches, etc.

Promote Peace...

So what are some practical ways that we can promote peace in our lives?

Just as the Israelites were missing a *piece* of their *peace*, we often are missing that *piece* of *peace*, too.

It has been said that we all have a God-shaped hole in our hearts. Augustine responds to that idea with these words: "Thou hast made us for Thyself, and our hearts are restless until they rest in Thee." He may have lived centuries ago, but Augustine had it right: when a God-shaped *piece* of us is missing, we won't have *peace* until we fill it with what - or Who - fits that hole, Jesus. When we try to fill it with other things, they don't fit, and we are still left empty.

So when a *piece* of us is missing *peace*, how do we fill the void of the God-shaped hole in our hearts?

Let us first say this: God never promised us a life of complete peace. In fact, He knew that there would be moments of heartache, grief, and uncertainty. He knew that we would have holes in our lives that would need to be filled. Too often, we try to fill those holes with other things in search of a state of peace. We don't realize that eirēnē is the answer to the void that we feel. We need the Prince of Peace. Jesus makes us whole and complete.

On the next page, we've given you some examples of things we typically run to for peace followed by things we *should* run to for peace. On the puzzle pieces, try some on your own.

Instead of busyness, find ways to spread peace around you.
Instead of jumping to social media, find answers in God's Word.
Instead of eating the house down, feed on God's truth.
Instead of numbing your mind with television, set your mind on things above.

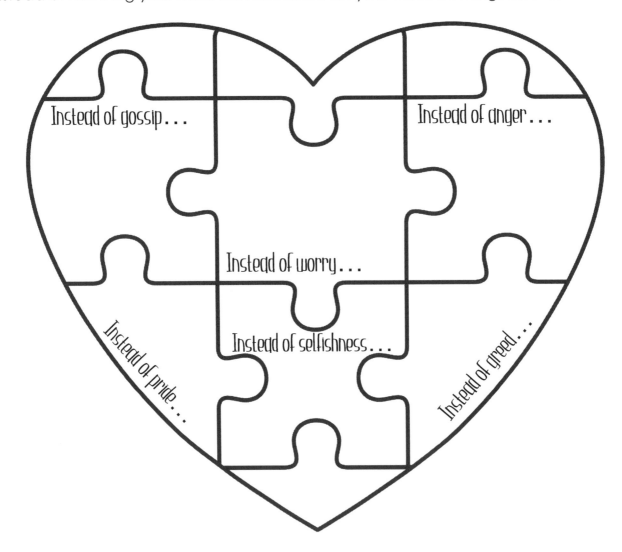

Instead of gossip...

Instead of anger...

Instead of worry...

Instead of selfishness...

Instead of pride...

Instead of greed...

The journey is not an easy one. We can promise that you will have moments of falter. Promoting peace in your life is a constant renewal of your heart and mind. We ain't gonna lie...we have struggled plenty of times with finding places of peace. 😄 However, we remember...

The missing **piece** is **peace**, and Jesus is the only **peace** that can fill the void that is within us.

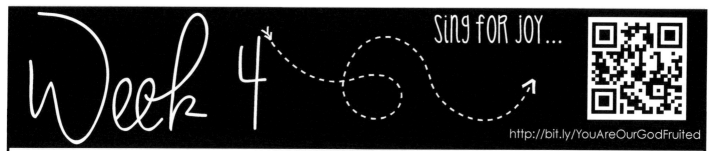

SCRIPTURE MEMORY: "Though the fig tree should not blossom, nor fruit be on the vines, the produce of the olive fail and the fields yield no food, the flock be cut off from the fold and there be no herd in the stalls, yet I will rejoice in the LORD; I will take joy in the God of my salvation." Habakkuk 3:17-18

Patience. I mean we know every teacher needs it, but some students require more of our patience than others. Would you agree? Surely you've had a student who just needed some extra doses of your patience...

Well, one particular year, I, Bonnie, needed more patience than I ever knew I'd need. I had a little girl enter my class who struggled greatly to adjust to the school experience. She had separation anxiety, and while we know that's not uncommon for kindergarten babies, her case was extreme. Her crying fits - and I *really* mean all out screaming matches - could last for hours...yes, plural...hours. Her crocodile tears and screaming were often accompanied by donkey kicks to the point where she would almost kick her friends.

I tried every trick in the book. I tried a sticker reward system. I tried a visual schedule. I tried candy rewards. I asked experienced teachers for their input and put their ideas into action but to no avail.

I was literally at wit's end. I knew she couldn't help it. Her poor little self just wasn't sure who she could trust. She didn't feel safe and secure...well, not yet.

I worked to build trust with her day in and day out. Eventually, about three weeks into the struggle, she began to settle down. Trust was built. Our days together actually began to be more enjoyable. Her smiles came more often than her tears. Her sweet little giggles replaced her screams.

It is not much different with us. God shows us much patience when we are the ones crying and kicking and screaming because our poor little selves don't feel safe and secure.

How do we find that trust and security? Well, by getting to know our loving Father and Savior and knowing that He is a safe place.

Just like my little friend learned in time to trust that I meant her no harm and that our room was a safe place, we will find in time as we spend time with Jesus that He means us no harm, only good, and that He is a safe place - a refuge in times in trouble.

50

patience

Fill in the blank.

"But the fruit of the Spirit is love, joy peace, _____, kindness, goodness, faithfulness, gentleness, and self control."
Galatians 5:22

If there is one trait that all teachers everywhere need if they're going to last in the classroom, it is patience. Can we get an amen?!😂

No education class can prepare you for hearing your name spoken and mispronounced 3,000 times before noon.

patience
(makrothymia)
noun

1. patience, endurance, constancy, steadfastness, perseverance
2. patience, forbearance, long-suffering, slowness in avenging wrongs
3. occurs 14 times

No amount of training can prepare you for the number of times you'll have to calmly look at Table 4 and say, "Now, we don't need our outside voices right now. Inside voices, please."

No student teaching adventure can prepare you for the middle school coma that seems to rob children of their ever-loving minds for three years or so. You know...the days where 30 times each class period you ask, "Where is your homework?" and the honest-to-goodness answer is "I don't know! I just had it!" and they REALLY do not know because the Middle School Monster ate it!? **#onlymiddleschoolteachersgetit**😳😄

No professional development adequately covers **#whenhighschoolersthinktheyareadults** or **#highschooldrama101** or **#highschoolattitudesolutionsthatwork**😳

I mean, good grief, y'all. If there were a patience vitamin, teachers would buy stock in it!

Soooo…is this the kind of patience Paul was instructing the Galatians to have? Well, not exactly.

You see, there are three Greek words for patience. Two come from the same root word – our word, makrothymia – that we see in Galatians 5:22. The other one is found in verses like Romans 8:25, Hebrews 12:1, James 1:3-4, etc. The word used in those verses is hypomonē. It means to "wait steadfastly; patiently wait." It's what we think of most often when we hear the word patience.

Turn to Hebrews 12:1. It's perhaps one of the most well-known uses of this Greek word.

Can you spot the word that has been translated from our Greek word, hypomonē?

If you guessed, endurance, you are correct!

While teaching requires this hypomonē kind of patience, I think we're about to find that teaching requires the makrothymia kind of patience, too.

Today, let's see what this kind of patience looks like with God.

Turn to Romans 2. Fair warning – Paul ain't too happy in this passage. 😅😮

Read verses 3 and 4.

Did you catch our word? It's in verse 4. Go back and re-read verse 4 to see if you can catch the variation in the meaning.

Take a guess…what do you think patience means in this context?

Matthew Henry defines makrothymia this way: "patience to defer anger and a contentedness to endure injuries."

Whoa. Ouch. Give us a moment to peel that foot off of our toes because man! 😵 That hurt!

A contentedness to endure injuries? We're supposed to be content to endure injuries?

Well...yes...yes, we are. We're going to get to what that looks like in our personal lives, but first, jump back to Romans 2:4 for a second. Hasn't God done the same with us? Isn't that what Paul is saying there?

Paul was showing the Romans – and us, too – that God has deferred His anger with humans. He has endured His own injuries...from us, in fact. We have, Bonnie and Bethany first and foremost, taken advantage of His patience, not recalling in our sinful, rebellious heart moments that He was drawing us to repentance with that kind patience of His.

Let's check out one other well-known story that demonstrates this makrothymia of God.

Turn to 1 Peter 3. Read verses 18-20.

Which popular Old Testament story is mentioned that reveals God's deferred anger?

| |
| |

The story of Noah is found in Genesis 7. We won't turn there and read it, but if you have time this week, spend some time in Genesis 6-9. You'll understand just how much patience God was showing the people of Noah's time.

But let's remember this: God did not act quickly to destroy all of humankind. He gave them chance after chance to come to repentance.

Write out 2 Peter 3:9 below.

| |
| |

Circle the word that indicates how many people God wants to reach repentance.

Oh friends, why is God so patient with us? Why does He show us so much makrothymia? As 2 Peter 3:15 says, we can "count the patience [the makrothymia] of our Lord as salvation..."

Perhaps now would be a good time to ask. Have you accepted Christ as the Lord of your life and allowed Him to be your Savior?

There is nothing you have done in your past that could ever outrun His patience. The very reason that He defers His judgment day after day is because He longs for you to turn to Him. If you haven't turned to Him, you can do that right now by simply admitting you are a sinner, asking Him for forgiveness for the sins that you have committed against Him, telling Him you believe that He sent His Son, Jesus, to die on the Cross for your sins, and telling Him that you want Him to be the Lord of your life. If that is something you did for the first time today, would you let someone know? We'd love to hear from you, but we'd also love for you to tell someone near you – a friend, a pastor, a loved one.

If you've already accepted Him as your Savior, is there an area of your life that you are "presuming on the riches of His...patience" as Paul said in Romans 2:4? In other words, are there areas of sin or rebellion that you are letting remain unchecked, knowing that you need to deal with them? Spend some time in prayer confessing that to the Father who loves you so dearly. Thank Him for His great patience toward us.

Dear Jesus,

Yesterday, we looked at the definition of our word for patience, makrothymia. We specifically looked at the idea of God's anger being deferred.

Do you remember the second part of the definition from Matthew Henry? If not, turn back, and write it below.

Personally, we find this part of the definition even more difficult to swallow. Deferring our anger is one thing. Enduring with contentedness an injury toward us is quite another. 😬

Let's look at another commentator's definition:

> "...a patient bearing and enduring of present evils with joyfulness... being slow to anger, ready to forgive injuries, put up with affronts, and bear with, and forbear one another..." (John Gill)

This definition reminds me, Bethany, of one of my all time favorite books of the Bible, James. I fell in love with this book when I was challenged to read it for a month straight back in my college days. It is amazing what truths you can glean when you just chew on the same bits of Scripture for days upon days. 😎

James is writing to the Jews who were dispersed all over during a rough patch of Jewish history. Many had lost everything and had been separated from family and friends. In this letter, he writes to them to tell them to "count it all joy...when you meet trials of various kinds, [knowing] that the testing of your faith produces steadfastness" (1:1-2). And if you guessed that "steadfastness" is also translated as "patience," you'd be right. It isn't makrothymia; however, it is hypomonē.

He goes on to tell them how to endure suffering in chapter 5 because many of them were enduring injuries, injustices, infirmities.

Turn to James 5 and read verses 7-11.

What Old Testament hero of the faith is mentioned in verse 11?

If anyone suffered wrongs for what seemed no reason at all, it was Job. He lost his house, his children, his flocks, his money, and eventually, even his wife turned against him.

You know what is amazing about Job, though? He got up under those trials and remained there. Job felt some very real, human emotions during that time, but Job 13:15a demonstrates his response to his sufferings.

Why don't you turn there and write it below.

Can you think of a time in your life that you suffered a wrong that really made no sense to you? Like Job, you were living "...blameless and upright...[fearing] God and [turning] away from evil..." (Job 1:1) yet it just seemed that life or certain people were against you?

Think or write about that time below.

When we think of Job's story, we see an example of the overall war that takes place on earth day in and day out...that invisible spiritual battle that is always waging. Satan wanted to test Job. Period. He went for the strongest link and thought he could pull Job down along with everyone around him. What happened was that everyone around Job fell, and Job stayed strong under the pressure of God's hand. He trusted that God had a purpose.

What's encouraging to us in this story is that Satan was not allowed to do anything – not one single thing – without God's permission. So when we are asked to endure an injury, it has passed through the hand of God first. With His strength, our weakness is made strong in Him because His grace is sufficient (2 Corinthians 12:9).

So what was the purpose of such an injury?

Turn to Job 42 and read verses 1 through 3.

You see, what Job realized is that God's ways are not His. When he began to question what God was allowing, he eventually understood that God's plans could not be fully comprehended by the human mind. His bottom line was "I learned to trust that you are God, and I am not."

Let's think of it this way: makrothymia produces in us hypomonē. In other words, when we learn to bear up under the injuries that are allowed into our lives, what is produced in us is a patient endurance. An endurance that lasts until we get the answer as to why the injury happened, which may not be until we reach the gate of heaven. An endurance that makes us trust that He is God and we are not. An endurance that bows heart and life to our Father.

As we both look back on times of "injury" in our lives, though we didn't recognize it at the time, what we see on the other side is that God's purpose was to show us where we were not like Him. Although we may have been living godly lives at the time, our response to the injuries often brings to the surface the ungodliness – the anger, the bitterness, the lashing out, the unlovingness, etc. – that still needs to be refined. When we can stop and say with Job, "I learned to trust that you are God, and I am not, and I still need You to shape me to reflect You," we will understand the purpose of those makrothymia times in our lives.

James 5:7-8 holds words that seem appropriate, not just for the Jews during the Diaspora, but also for us in moments where we are bearing up under injuries that we do not understand:

"Be patient, therefore, brothers [and sisters], until the coming of the Lord…Establish your hearts, for the coming of the Lord is at hand."

We must counsel our hearts and remind ourselves that God allows nothing into our lives for our harm. If we are asked to endure hardship, He will bring good from it (Romans 8:28).

Spend a few minutes listening to this beautiful reminder from Kari Jobe as you color.

http://bit.ly/BeStillMySoulFruited

Have you ever squeezed a grape and had orange juice come out? Or how about a grapefruit...did lemon juice come out? **#obviouslyno #yallareweird** 😜

We may be weird, and that may be a weird question, but it's a fair one for this week. When push comes to shove – or perhaps we should say when juicer is applied to fruit 😆 – whatever kind of fruit you squeeze, the same kind of juice is comin' out. Oranges give orange juice. Lemons give lemon juice. Grapes give grape juice. The end.

The same is true with us. When situations squeeze us, what comes out proves who we really are. Hope you've joined us in wearing steel-toed boots for the next few moments, because...well...here we go... 😄 Truth time, y'all!

...if someone not pressing their gas pedal the first millisecond the light turns green squeezes anger out of us, we might need that situation until makrothymia comes out.

...if standing in the grocery store line for more than 45 seconds squeezes sighs and rolling eyes out of us, we might need that situation until makrothymia comes out.

...if that student tapping his pencil squeezes, "STOP THAT RIGHT NOW!" out of us, we might need that situation until makrothymia comes out.

...if corny jokes from that one middle school boy squeezes annoyance out of us, we might need that situation until makrothymia comes out.

...if one more email from our administrator squeezes a bad attitude out of us, we might need that situation until makrothymia comes out.

You see, makrothymia situations prove who we really are. The goal is that when we are squeezed by situations that we do not understand in the least bit, what comes out is love, joy, peace, patience, kindness, goodness, faithfulness, gentleness, and self control.

We don't know about you, but we're not there yet!

Be honest – what are the top 3 "juices" that come out when life squeezes you a little too hard in all the "right" places?

I, Bethany, used to be an incredibly angry person. No, I'm not kidding though I wish I were. 😳 I'm talking the kind of anger that is set off by any little thing. You looked at me wrong? Gonna yell. Your tone makes me think you're putting me down in some way? Gonna scream. You hurt my feelings? Gonna stomp away...far away...and let you know I'm mad. Honestly, rather embarrassing to admit to you, but it's the ugly truth of my sin, y'all.

I used to beg the Lord to take away my anger because behind closed doors, I knew it was wrong. In fact, I wept over it most nights. It was like I didn't know how to control it. I couldn't fix it. I wanted to fix it, but I just couldn't figure out how.

I stumbled upon Psalm 107:20 during that time. Why don't you turn there and write it below.

It was one of those light bulb moments for me. I needed more of God's Words in me before the anger could be squeezed out of me. It also occurred to me that every time I was in a situation that squeezed me, it was occurring to squeeze all that ugliness right out of me, only I wasn't responding correctly.

The more time I spent in God's Word, the more I was able to see Him transforming me. Situations that used to make me angry no longer had quite the same effect. My response was different. Now, I look back on those years and think, "Who was that?!?!?"😮😳

Let's spend the rest of today being Bible scholars. If it is God's Word that heals, we need to find places in God's Word that speak to our volatile areas.

List the 3 areas below that you want to work on demonstrating patience – makrothymia – most in your life.

①

②

③

Can you think of at least one example of a situation or a person that is in your life right now that God is most likely using to help work on one of the above areas while He teaches you to have makrothymia and bear up under that struggle?

Biblestudytools.com is one of our favorite websites to use when writing or studying. It is a great library of various versions of the Bible, commentaries, messages, etc. Using that site, or another one of your favorite sites, search verses that speak to the three areas you wrote on the previous page. (You can also simply Google "verses about anger," "verses about impatience," "verses about bitterness," etc.) Write the verses on or around the grapes. You have the license to be creative.

DaY 4 → DON'T Be Rotten

You know what language we hate the most? Christianese. Is that a thing, you may be asking? Why, yes, yes, it is! 😄

Defined: Christianese is using words from the Bible or from the Christian realm that we really don't understand or have a grasp on practically speaking. (Examples: sanctification, guard your heart...) Though it's incredibly important for us to understand these words, we oftentimes jump over them without really digging deep and understanding them.

So, today, let's get practical. Let's ditch the Christianese of our definitions this week and figure out what it looks like to live with makrothymia.

The first part of our definition was **"deferring anger."**

The word deferring is defined as "putting off to a later time; postpone."

Let's first ask the question, when squeezed by a situation or a person, how does putting off our anger until later help the situation? What is most likely going to happen?

You left your kids with a sub because you had professional development. You came back to a classroom that was all but destroyed. 😳 Chairs out of place. Some turned over, in fact. Papers everywhere as though a tornado had hit right at dismissal time. Work? What work? They did no work! A table was broken. The sub note basically said they were okay but could use some structure. Immediate reaction? AHHHHHHHHHHHHHHH! Steam coming out of your ears. 😠

If you wouldn't respond to that in anger, you are more godly than we are. How frustrating is that situation? How real is that situation!?

DAY 4 DON'T BE ROTTEN

Let's add to that scenario: let's say you returned on a Friday, but Friday was a teacher workday, so you won't see those angels again until Monday. By the time you see them again Monday, has your anger and frustration cooled at all? If you didn't stew on it all weekend, if you practiced deferred anger, probably so.

When we defer our anger, we don't stew on a situation that makes us mad. We don't keep thinking about it minute after minute. We put it away. We give it to the Lord. We ask Him to help us know how to deal with the situation, and we LEAVE it with Him and walk away from it. When we can truly do that, our anger begins to fizzle out most times. Our perspective usually changes. We may realize that we were about to over-react.

Deferred anger is when we postpone anger until we can decide if it's righteous anger or not.

We've listed an example of a situation that would be considered righteous anger and an example that would be ungodly anger. Can you add an example of each?

Righteous Anger: You discovered a parent was physically abusing a child in your class.

Ungodly Anger: A student broke one of your flexible seating chairs and hid it from you, and you just found out. ☺

Righteous Anger

Ungodly Anger

DaY 4 DoN't bE RottEN

When we are squeezed, if makrothymia is coming out, we will defer our anger long enough to decide if it's righteous anger or not. If it isn't righteous, we'll drop it. If it is righteous, then we'll take necessary actions to see God's ways exalted.

The second part of our definition was **"to endure injuries with contentedness."**

This was a little more "ouch" inducing than the first. How in the world do we endure injuries with joy? 😮

...the parent that berates us almost daily in emails or face-to-face because we are obviously what is wrong with his or her child. *We are the reason the child is failing.*

...the student who yells at us, throws things at us, disrespects us in every way shape or form even though we go out of our way to help him or her.

...the administrator who never has anything kind to say to us and never notices the good things we do, yet is quick to point out every single thing we do wrong.

...the coworker who gossips about us and thinks we never hear it – or maybe they know we hear it, but they don't care because they simply don't like us.

How do we bear those injuries with joy?

Turn to Psalm 37.

David is in his later years here. He has spent so much of his life enduring injuries. He has watched the wicked getting away with their wrongs – or so it seemed at times. Yet in his old age, he has finally discovered truth: a reason to endure with joy.

Read verses 6-11.

Write verse 6 below.

65

DAY 4 ~ DON'T bE ROTTEN

When we are living rightly, God sees that. Even if everyone else believes that parent…that student…that administrator…that coworker…God knows. In His timing, "He will bring forth your righteousness as the light…" As surely as the sun comes out at noon every day, people will see truth. He will be sure of it.

Have you ever let a piece of fruit rot? Do you know that though it stinks for a while, it eventually decays – to the point of crumbling and turning to dust again if you leave it long enough?

That is what happens to the rotten "fruit" that speaks injuries over us. They may stink for a while – maybe even a loooooooong while. But eventually, they go away because they aren't truth. Don't let rotten fruit spoil the fruit that you are called to bear. When rotten fruit tries to come along side your good fruit and spoil it, don't let it. Instead, respond with makrothymia.

Pray for that rotten fruit.

Take refuge in the shelter of the Almighty, and let the Almighty use all of His might to take care of them.

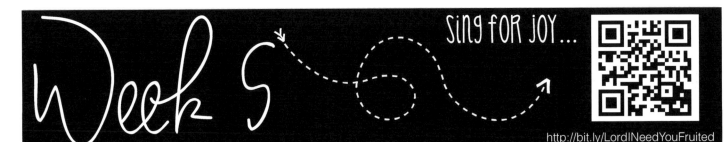

SCRIPTURE MEMORY: "...that Christ may dwell in your hearts through faith – that you, being rooted and grounded in love, may have strength to comprehend with all the saints what is the breadth and length and height and depth, and to know the love of Christ that surpasses knowledge, that you may be filled with all the fullness of God." Ephesians 3:17-19

Let me, Bethany, take you back to my first middle school classroom. Bright turquoise, yellow, and black dots bedazzled the tops of my walls - you know the re-positionable ones that were oh so popular in the early 2000s? I had zero clue what I was doing. I felt like a fish out of water. These middle schoolers were crazyyyyyy, and they were way too close to my age for comfort...or so it felt back then.

I quickly learned that middle school = drama...no truer equation exists. I had to find a way to subvert such nasty and catty behaviors, particularly with the girls, or we'd never make it out of the year alive! Me included!

One day in Bible, we came across Proverbs 25:22. (Go ahead and read it...it's a good one.) The girls had a marvelous idea! We were going to work on "heaping coals of kindness" on our enemies' heads rather than getting even. So they vowed that the next time someone made them mad, they'd write the person a card or give them some candy...anonymously, of course. I kept a box of cards in my room for this express purpose and stocked my mini classroom store with candy, too. It really worked like a charm. Now, let's be real...had it been my idea? It would've failed. Because it was their idea, they bought into it hook, line, and sinker. Win!

But that wasn't it. Their kindness started to flow over into their every day thoughts and actions. Every year at Christmas, I threw them a Christmas party. We had a "Happy Birthday, Jesus" cake, pizza, chips, drinks, gifts...the whole shebang.

This same year - the year of kindness - they came to me and asked if they could do something in place of their party. I looked at them a little confused and asked what they had in mind. Y'all, they had raised money - hundreds of dollars! - to give to a needy family. There was a family with 3 kids living in a hotel. Sad situation. These middle school babies brought in bikes, clothes, toys, food - you name it, they brought it. We wrapped everything and took a field trip. The whole way there, these 8th graders sang Christmas carols. I've never seen such glowing faces. We arrived and crammed all 30+ bodies into the tiny room. We laughed. We cried. The family laughed. They cried.

We left that day different people. They've never forgotten it. Those once middle schoolers are now turning 23-24 years old. They still text me about it. Why? Because kindness changes people - especially the giver.

Fill in the blank.

"But the fruit of the Spirit is love, joy
  peace, patience, _____ , goodness,
  faithfulness, gentleness, and self control."
  Galatians 5:22

kindness
(chrēstotēs)
noun
1. moral goodness, integrity
2. benignity, kindness
3. occurs 8 times

"Throw kindness around like confetti." We know you've heard that quote before. You may even have it on your bulletin board! 😎

We are going to be honest - like we would EVER lie to you - when we think of that statement, it makes us think, *What teacher in her right mind would ever throw confetti around in the classroom?* 😂

Here is how this scenario would go...

Teacher: "Here, children, throw this confetti around the classroom!"

Children act like crazy people and throw confetti. Insert utter chaos!

Teacher: "Your kindness should be thrown around just like this confetti."
Children: "Say what?!? Huh?"
Teacher: "Now, your kindness toward me will be to pick up ALL this confetti."

Let it be known - Bethany and Bonnie ain't gonna be throwin' any kinda confetti around in our classrooms. **#iaintdoinit** 😂

DAY 1 ~ Kindness confetti

While we tease about that quote...not so much teasing about not wanting such a confetti mess in our classrooms! 😜 ...the theme of kindness is sprinkled all throughout Scripture. The meta-narrative of Scripture, simply defined as looking at Scripture as a whole from Genesis to Revelation, is filled to the brim with example after example of God's more-than-generous doses of kindness toward His creation.

Romans 2:4b gives us the purpose behind His kindness toward us. Paul says that "...God's kindness is meant to lead us to repentance." Kindness has a way of melting hardened hearts.

We don't know about you, but if you've ever had someone treat you with kindness when you know you didn't deserve it, you know that it makes you stop in your tracks and contemplate why they would treat you that way.

God the Father does that with us. He has shown us such kindness. Before He ever breathed the world into existence, He planned out each of our days. He planned long before Creation to send His One and Only Son to die for humans that He knew would reject Him. We did absolutely nothing to deserve His kindness. In fact, we did everything to deserve quite the opposite, but His love for us is sprinkled on us moment-by-moment in the form of kindness. When we realize how little we deserve yet how much He has given, we are brought to repentance.

Below, write some examples of God's kindness that He sprinkles over your life each day.

69

DAY 1 ~ Kindness confetti

Sometimes it is hard to see God's kindness in the difficulties of our days. Trials come. Hardships loom. Gray clouds cover our days. We begin to wonder, *God, where is Your kindness in all of this?*

We begin to blame God.
We begin to wonder if God loves us.
We begin to believe we are not deserving of His kindness.
We begin to criticize ourselves, saying, "Of course God isn't going to be kind to me because I am _____." (You fill in the blank.)

Lies. Lies. All lies!

Trials are not God's fault, but He does allow them for our growth and His glory.
God does love us - so much that He sent His Only Son for us.
There is nothing we can do to earn or lose God's kindness.
God loves us just the way we are - bumps, bruises, and beauty marks.

When our thought patterns about God and His kindness begin to reflect the lies rather than the truth, we need to be reminded to be kind to ourselves because God is kind to us.

Take a minute to reflect on ways that you may not be so kind to yourself.

Andrew Peterson, a popular singer and songwriter, began to notice these erroneous - and dangerous - thought patterns in his daughter. He sat down one night and wrote a song to remind her that she needed to see herself through her daddy's eyes rather than her not-quite-clear and not-fully-developed eyes.

The message he was giving to his baby girl is the same one our Father is giving to us: be kind to yourself...because I love you just the way that you are.

Scan the QR code or follow the bit.ly link to listen to Andrew Peterson's song, "Be Kind to Yourself."

http://bit.ly/BeKindtoYourselfFruited

Let's take a moment to remember who we are in Christ so that we can ditch the lies we've been believing and re-wallpaper our minds with truth (Romans 12:2).

You are **created** in the image of God. (Genesis 1:27)
You are **loved** with an everlasting love. (Jeremiah 31:3)
You are **adopted** by the God of the Universe. (John 1:12-13)
You are **alive** with Christ. (Galatians 2:20)
You are **accepted** by Christ. (Romans 15:7)
You are **united** with Christ. (1 Corinthians 6:17)
You are **set apart** by God. (1 Peter 1:16)
You are **a part of the body of Christ**. (1 Corinthians 12:27)
You are **God's workmanship**. (Ephesians 2:10)
You are **a child of God**. (1 John 3:1-2)

Is it just us, or do you sometimes find it difficult to be kind? We know our students have a hard time being kind.

For a teacher, it might be hard to be kind when...

...a student asks, "What am I supposed to do on this page?" for the 100th time.
...a student runs and flips and crashes into another student.
...a parent emails you in the heat of the moment and says some not-so-nice things.
...an administrator walks into your classroom unannounced and harshly critiques what you're doing.
...a co-worker leaves the copier jammed or without paper.
...a parent undermines your requests as a teacher.
...a student cops an attitude with you.

Can you add to our list?

... _____

... _____

... _____

Kindness ain't easy! ☺ However, it should be our response to God's kindness toward us.

Remember back to the beginning of our study when we talked about the Galatians believing a different gospel than what Paul preached to them? They weren't exactly being kind to one other, but rather were fighting and arguing and bickering over who was right and who was wrong.

Look up Ephesians 4:32 and Colossians 3:12 and write them below.

Soooooo where was this kindness that Paul instructed the Galatians and the Ephesians and the Colossians to put on and throw around like confetti? Missing. They were really good at throwing around confusion and chaos, though. Sound familiar? 😬

Go back and look at the list we just created. When we respond to those situations incorrectly and unkindly, chaos and confusion erupt.

It's really easy to respond incorrectly to situations like those because those are the people and things that annoy us the most. **#amiright** 😅

However, we do not get extra credit for being kind to kind people like…the good student, the gracious co-worker, the encouraging administrator, the supportive parent. It's easy to be kind to kind people…but the not-so-kind? Yikes!

Read Luke 6:32-36.

Being kind to our enemies is not a natural response. It is a Holy Spirit inspired response. **#fruited** In order to respond in these situations with kindness, we must be rooted in God's Word and His Truth.

Read Proverbs 25:21-22.

What metaphor (comparison) is being made in verse 22?

In Biblical times, when a blacksmith was working with metal and needed to re-shape it, he would pile burning coals on top of the metal to make it more malleable. The more coals he piled on it, the faster it would heat up and the more easily it could be re-shaped. This is precisely the metaphor that we find in Proverbs 25. Kindness has the ability to warm up cold hearts and make them more receptive.

Before we run to this as a quick fix method, let's discuss what this metaphor is **not** saying.

It does **not** mean that I'm going to be kind to my administrator one time, and he or she will all of a sudden be on my side.

It does **not** mean that going the extra mile and sending a sweet note home one time is going to cause a parent to be immediately supportive.

It does **not** mean that being nice to a grumpy co-worker will change his or her attitude when you meet him or her in the teacher's lounge the next day.

It does **not** mean that if you choose to be kind to a student that gets under your skin, that student will not annoy you again.

What it **does** mean is that as we bear the fruit of kindness long term, we will see the fruits of our labor because the Lord rewards our obedience to Him.

It is more about **our growth** than it is **their change in behavior.**
It is more about **our becoming more like Christ** than it is **their becoming less difficult.**
It is more about **our relationship with Jesus** than it is **their relationship with us**.

Take some time to think and pray for people in your life that make it difficult to be kind. After your prayer time, list some practical ways you can show kindness toward them.

goodness

Fill in the blank.

"But the fruit of the Spirit is love, joy
peace, patience, kindness, _____ ,
faithfulness, gentleness, and self control."
Galatians 5:22

goodness
(agathōsynē)
noun

1. uprightness of heart and life, goodness, kindness
2. occurs 4 times

Did reading the definition for the word *goodness* seem a little like déjà vu? It did for us! In fact, in all transparency, as we studied these two oh-so-similarly-defined words, we struggled to separate them.

After much study and contemplation, the simplest way to describe the difference is this: Kindness flows out of our salvation. It is an attitude by which we live because of what Jesus did for us. Goodness is the active version of kindness. It is the hands and legs and feet to the body of kindness. Goodness is an extension of kindness.

Turn back and read your list from the end of yesterday. By these definitions, that is really your list of goodness acts, not kindness acts. Ever heard of **#randomactsofkindness**? Those really should be **#randomactsofgoodness**! 😄

Sooo let's go back to the root of this word...**#nopunintended** The root word for goodness is agathos. One of the places in Scripture that the root word is used is Matthew 7. Let's take a look at the passage beginning in verse 15 and ending in verse 20.

DAY 3 — Taste and See

From the outside, it is often easy to believe that something that looks good is good. Please tell us we are not the only ones who have made this mistake before. 😬 However, what Jesus is warning us in this passage is that we must test the fruit in order to know the root.

You get bonus points if you can recall what kind of false prophets (or teachers) the Galatians encountered that Paul warned should not be allowed to integrate into the Galatia churches. What were these false teachers teaching? (If you must, you may look back. Bethany says that's **#cheating**. Bonnie says that's using **#textevidence**.) 😆

According to Matthew 7:16, how do we distinguish between false teachers and godly teachers?

Many years ago, Bonnie dated a guy, who was the pastor of a small, local church. She jumped into this relationship with both feet, completely trusting that he was a good, godly guy. The more she got to know him and the longer she was in the relationship, certain behaviors began to pop up that made her question the validity of his trustworthiness. What he had claimed was part of his past was, in fact, part of his present lifestyle - a lifestyle of alcohol and drugs. What originally looked like a good, healthy tree turned out to be the bad, diseased tree Matthew 7 is describing. It was his fruit that began to give away the fact that his root was rotten.

Deceptive fruit actually goes waaaaaaaaay back to Genesis. The serpent used the beautiful, ripe fruit to deceive Eve into believing that its roots were good for her. The fruit was tempting, but once she bit that fruit, she realized that with it came separation, destruction, alienation, heartache, sorrow, pain, and loneliness. 😞

Back to Bonnie's story…it was by God's grace and His protection that she was snatched out of the relationship before the roots of the relationship grew too deep.

When the root of our relationship with Christ is strong enough and deep enough, He will give us the discernment we need to distinguish between what is a good fruit and what is a bad fruit.

The Galatians were dealing with a lotta bad apples. These false teachers appeared good on the outside, but their roots were bruised and rotten. Paul warned the Galatians to test what these people were saying against the true Gospel of Jesus that he had preached to them.

76

By the time he penned the words of Galatians 5:22-23, Paul was reminding the Galatians how desperately they needed this Fruit of the Spirit so that they would stand out. This fruit would allow others around them to know they belonged to Jesus.

Our acts of goodness are a way that our lives can proclaim Whose we are. We belong to Jesus, and everything we do should show the world around us that we are rooted and grounded in Him. Our fruit is sweet; it is good. Every time someone takes a bite of our fruit, they should be able to taste God's goodness and see for themselves that He is good.

Oh taste and see that the LORD is good.

Psalm 34:8

gentleness

Fill in the blank.

"But the fruit of the Spirit is love, joy peace, patience, kindness, goodness, faithfulness, _____, and self control."
Galatians 5:22

Bonus points for the person who can figure out what fruit we just skipped...easiest bonus points of your life! 😂

**gentleness
(praÿtēs)
noun**
1. mildness of disposition, gentleness of spirit, meekness
2. occurs 11 times

Admittedly, it was a mistake on our part. When writing this study, we didn't write about the Fruit of the Spirit in order, sooooo it was an easy mistake to make as we wrote where God led us each writing day. When we realized the mistake, we were 85-90% done with the study, which means it was nearly impossible to fix the error without changing the layout of our weeks. **#aintnobodygottimeforthat** 😮

However, sometimes God uses our mistakes for His purposes. As we took a walk and started talking through it, it actually seemed to be something that God designed even though we didn't realize it.

You see, kindness is the attitude we are to have. Goodness is the actions behind the kindness. Gentleness is the way or manner in which the actions are presented. You see how perfectly that fits together? **#Godisawesome** 😎

DAY 4 — GENTLENESS

We have a coworker that is the very image of gentleness. When both of us think of this trait, she pops into our minds immediately. Ask any of our other coworkers, and we are confident they'd say the same.

Over the past couple of years, she has had some of the toughest groups of kids in her classroom. Quick caveat: don't get us wrong - we have great kids in our school. We are blessed to have the ones we have, but as every teacher knows, certain mixtures of certain personalities create a dynamic that is...well...less than desirable. However, despite the dynamics of her classroom, she has stayed the sweetest, most gentle teacher. I mean when we grow up, we just want to be like her.

She exudes sweetness. It's like her words drip with the honey of Jesus' love. Picture a kid running down the hall. We might say, "Stop running! Stop it right now!" She might simply walk up beside the child, motioning with her hand ever so gently, and the child would stop. It's like even after she gets onto you, you leave empowered and desiring to do better. Her words aren't down putting. They're truthful, but they're loving. She corrects in gentleness. The volume of her voice and the tone in which she speaks is gentle.

She lives in humility. Despite what's going on in her own world, her own classroom, she always stops to ask what is going on in our world. In fact, if she were reading this right now, she would smile sweetly, shake her head, and say, "Oh no, that's not me" and mean every word.

She's the person everyone wants as a friend. She's the person everyone wants to be when they grow up. She is a picture of Jesus.

Write below what comes to mind when you hear the word gentleness.

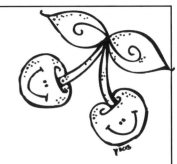

It is an unfortunate thing that our society has decided that gentleness is a negative quality. Many today would define gentleness as someone who gets walked all over or pushed down easily. Biblical gentleness is not that at all!

A simple definition of biblical gentleness is "power under control." Gentleness is not a wishy-washy quality of a person who is indecisive. It's not someone who gets pushed around by others and never speaks their opinions. It's a person whose actions and words are laced with love and respect as she lives her life serving others and interacting with others.

Look up Matthew 11:28-30. Notice how Jesus describes Himself in verse 29. Write His description of Himself below.

```



```

That same Jesus, who said "I am gentle," is seen in Matthew 21:12-13. Read those verses and tell us in a sentence or two what Jesus was doing.

```




```

You see, gentleness doesn't mean never speaking up. Gentleness doesn't mean getting walked all over or put down. Gentleness is power under control. When Jesus found His Father's home being used as a Jewish Market where the sellers were taking advantage of the people and making money off of them, He was angry - and rightfully so. He spoke up all right. He was not about to allow the money changers and salespeople to take advantage of His Father's house. He was righteously angry.

It is right for us to be angry about child prostitution.
It is right for us to be angry about Christians being murdered for their faith.
It is right for us to be angry about child abuse.

And when we see things like that happening, we should speak up! But do we lose our cool? No. We speak truth in love with power and boldness.

So...

...instead of responding in frustration and anger to the student who has asked a question that we've already answered 18 times, we should respond with gentle truth in a loving tone.

...instead of responding in frustration and anger to the parent who won't honor a request we've made, we still treat them with gentleness, not changing the tone or attitude we use when talking to them.

...instead of responding in frustration and anger to the administrator who continually steps on our toes and pushes our buttons, we respond to them with gentleness and continue to do our job well.

Spend some time in prayer, asking the Lord how you can be more gentle in some present situations that may be trying your gentleness.

Dear Jesus,

There are just some students who stand out from others. Some that perhaps stand a little taller. Stand out a little more...and they don't mind if they do because the reason they're standing that way is because they're standing for what's right.

It doesn't take my mind any more than 15 seconds to come up with two students that fit that description. Both are students who trust firmly in God's Word. It is evident that both of these girls devote their days to reading, if not, devouring God's Word. Both girls often probe into the depths of the riches of God's Word, pulling out treasures that many adults would not have uncovered at such a young age.

As you can imagine, both of these girls stand out in the crowd of their peers. Some of their peers aren't quite sure what to do with them. They are fine to isolate themselves from a crowd that is doing something that doesn't quite flow with their beliefs. Backlash doesn't bother them so much these days because they know that Jesus' opinion matters more than those criticizing them for their stand.

These girls are faithful. No matter the circumstance, no matter the consequence, they are going to choose to be faithful to what they believe.

Faithfulness isn't always the popular place to visit. It's often quite the lonely place...especially in today's culture. Faithfulness isn't really so useful in the easy times; it's really for the hard times. When the tough situations arise, it's faithfulness that gives us the grit to buckle down and hold on tight.

It's what kept Jesus clinging to His Father's will. It's what kept Mary believing that God would vindicate her as a virgin who found herself miraculously pregnant. It's what kept the disciples preaching Jesus Christ crucified when all around them threatened death if they spoke up one. more. time. It's what should keep us choosing right when no one else around is watching or following. It's what keeps these girls strong when all their peers think they're crazy for being so into what the Bible says.

Faithfulness is the fruit whose chorus rings out: "Though none go with me, still I will follow. Though none go with me, still I will follow. Though none go with me, still I will follow. No turning back. No turning back."

faithfulness

Fill in the blank.

"But the fruit of the Spirit is love, joy
peace, patience, kindness, goodness,

_____, gentleness, and self control."

Galatians 5:22

faithfulness
(Greek: pistis)
noun
1. the character of one
   who can be relied on
2. occurs 244 times

faithfulness
(Hebrew:
'emuwnah)
noun

1. fidelity, firmness,
   steadfastness,
   steadiness
2. occurs 48 times

As teachers, we're supposed to like apple stuff, right? We do. We like apple pie and Apple products, apple-scented candles and apple bulletin boards. Sooo in light of our teacher love for all things apple, we thought we'd let you go apple pickin' today. 😊

The New Testament was originally written in Greek. The Old Testament was originally written in Hebrew. Despite the two different languages, most words in the New Testament have an Old Testament match. This is the case with our word for this week, faithfulness.

In order to understand what faithfulness should look like in our lives, we first must understand how God has demonstrated His faithfulness to us. We need to see it first in Him since He is the One we are to imitate. To do this, we want you to go apple pickin' in the Old Testament.

Pick a few apples from our tree on the next page to help you get a taste of God's faithfulness. Around the tree, write out a few of the verses. We know you'll taste and see that He is good because it is true: His love and faithfulness endure forever!

Day 1 — Apple Pickin'

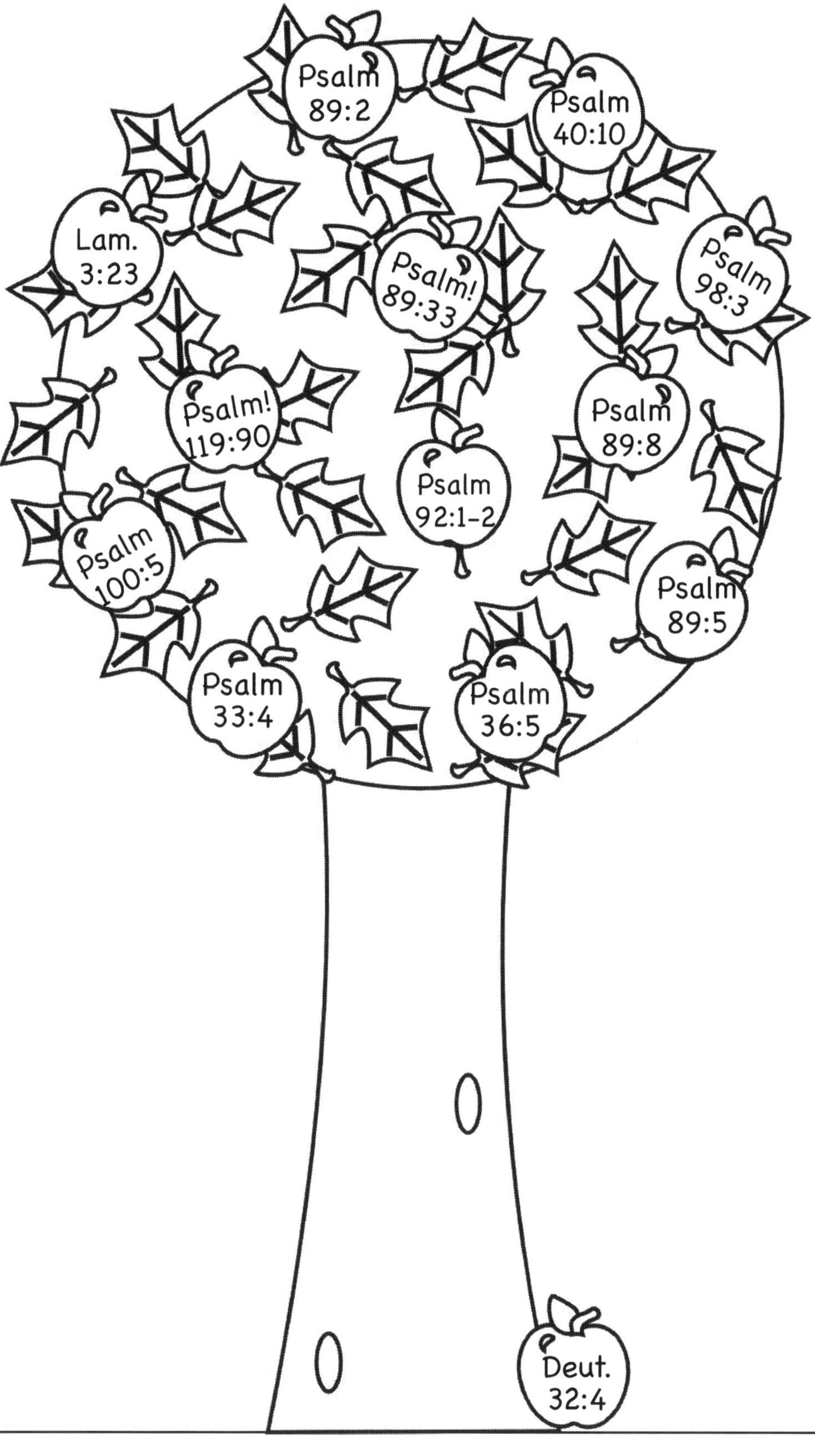
Psalm 89:2
Psalm 40:10
Lam. 3:23
Psalm 89:33
Psalm 98:3
Psalm 119:90
Psalm 89:8
Psalm 92:1-2
Psalm 100:5
Psalm 89:5
Psalm 33:4
Psalm 36:5
Deut. 32:4

The roots of that apple tree are supernaturally strong. They can never be broken. Nothing can move them. The same God who spoke trees into existence - roots and all - in Genesis 1:11-13 is the very same God who sent His Son, Jesus, who is the Root (Revelation 22:16) that connects us back to His Father, the Ever Faithful One.

God was **faithful** to Noah and his family during the flood. (Genesis 6-9)
God was **faithful** to Joseph when He turned what Joseph's brothers meant for evil into good. (Genesis 37-47)
God was **faithful** to Moses and the Israelites when He led them out of Egypt's captivity. (Exodus 1-14)
God was **faithful** to Rahab when He saved her family from destruction because she helped the Israelites. (Joshua 2 & 6)
God was **faithful** to Ruth when He provided a kinsman redeemer for her. (Ruth 1-4)
God was **faithful** to Job when he lost his health, family, and money. (Job 1-42)
God was **faithful** to Daniel when He saved him from the lions in the lions' den. (Daniel 6)

Now it's your turn. Think of one more example of God's faithfulness from Scripture. Then think of an example of God's faithfulness in your own life.

God was **faithful**

God was **faithful**

When we are frail of heart and have no hope within, we need to remember the Faithful One. Take a few moments to listen to the song, "Faithful One," by Selah as you reflect on God's perfect faithfulness.

http://bit.ly/FaithfulOneFruited

85

Behaviors elicit a response. The way a student behaves - good or bad - elicits a response from the teacher. The way the teacher responds - good or bad - elicits a response from the students.

Just like the classroom, God's faithfulness to us, His children, demands a response. So what does that response look like? Well, it looks like faithfulness. We are to respond by being faithful to Him and to what He has called us to do where He has called us to do it.

Let's spend some time with David in Psalm 37 today. Go ahead and turn there and read the entire chapter. Yep. We said it...the entire chapter. 😊

Look back at verse 1. Whom are we not to fret? _____

There were many times in David's life when he was surrounded by evildoers, people who were not being faithful to God. In fact, many of these evildoers were flat out non-Christians, and so the way they behaved was...well, just plain evil. 😨

In verses 3-4, David gives 5 commands - or 5 responses - we are to have even when the circumstances around us seem bleak, and the people around us have a totally different agenda.

Go ahead and write verses 3-4 below and then underline the 5 commands/responses. (Hint: There are 4 in verse 3, and there is 1 in verse 4.)

Let's look briefly at each response from those verses.

- **Trust** in the LORD: The Hebrew word that is used here is batach. It simply means to be carefree in the LORD, knowing that He is sovereign over everything and everyone.

- **Do** good: This is another fruit of the Spirit that we've already discussed - goodness. In the midst of all types of circumstances, we are to do good to those around us.

- **Dwell** in the land: We must admit - this is a hard one. 😮 The Hebrew word for dwell is shakan. Simply put, it means "to settle down; to abide; to reside." Let's get even more simplistic - wherever God has asked us to put down roots, we're to settle in as though we're going to stay awhile. It is SOOOO easy to look around us, see circumstances that are at best unpleasant and at worst downright unbearable, see people that we just don't mesh with, and say, "The grass has gotta be greener over there. I'm moving!" But what David is telling us from experience is that we are to be faithful in the midst of the desert seasons of life, our wilderness experiences, just as we are to be faithful when things around us are beautiful and going swell. Call us crazy, but that Hebrew word reminds us of our English word "shaken"...not in definition, but in spelling. You know what response this command should elicit from us? The very opposite of being shaken. We are to settle in and dwell where God has placed us, knowing that we can batach Him - we can be carefree in Him - because He knows exactly what the area around us is like. He has a plan. He has a purpose for where we are. Instead of being shaken, shakan.

> Write or think about a time in your life when you thought the grass might be greener on the other side.

- **Befriend** faithfulness: The Hebrew word for befriend is ra'ah. It is translated "feed" 75 times and "shepherd" 63 times. In times of difficulty, when those bleak circumstances appear and those people pop up with their personal agendas, we are to shepherd ourselves with God's promises, His truth. We are to feed on His faithfulness. We are to devour His Words and allow them to bring joy and rejoicing back into our hearts (Jeremiah 15:16). His faithfulness throughout Scripture and His faithfulness to us in our personal lives should give us hope as we trust that He will prove His faithfulness to us once again because He Who is Faithful cannot be unfaithful. Faithful is just Who He is.

> Jot down a verse or a story about God's faithfulness that could remind you of truth when you need help remembering that He is Faithful.

- **Delight** yourself in the LORD: What we love about these verses is that they build one on another. However, what we also know is that it's hard to jump to this one if we haven't truly obeyed and responded to the other four. When we are carefree in the LORD, knowing He's sovereign, and we're in turn doing good to others because God is good to us, when we are content to do what He's called us to do where He's called us to do it, and we're feeding on a steady diet of His past faithfulness to us, we will find that our joy is full because of Him. Our entire outlook changes. What once looked like a desert - barren, broken, and bleak - will become our home that is filled with hope, heart, and happiness. We will find that our heart's desires have been given to us in the exact place we thought all hope was lost.

> How do you think delighting yourself in the LORD would change your outlook in a present situation?

You see, what David realized as he looked back on his life was that God's faithfulness elicited a response of faithfulness from him, and when David responded with faithfulness, God gave him his heart's desire (vs. 4b), showed the ones against him that he was innocent and righteous (vs. 6), upheld him with His hand (vs. 24), and remained his stronghold (vs. 39). God's faithfulness elicits our faithfulness.

Not only does God's faithfulness elicit a response from us, but our faithfulness to Him elicits a response from Him: **His benefits.**

Let's look at 5 benefits that God gives to us when we are faithful. Look up the following verses and fill in the blanks.

 Psalm 37:28a - "For the LORD loves justice; he will _____ _____ His faithful ones..."

 Proverbs 3:12 - "My son, do not forget my teaching, but let your heart keep my commandments, for _____ of days and _____ of life and peace they will add to you."

DAY 2 — OUR RESPONSE

3 Proverbs 16:6-7 - "By steadfast love and faithfulness iniquity is atoned for, and by the fear of the LORD one turns away from evil. When a man's ways please the LORD, he makes even his _____ to be at _____ with him."

4 Proverbs 28:20a - "A faithful man will abound with _____ ..."

5 Revelation 2:10c - "...Be faithful unto death, and I will give you the _____ _____ _____ ."

Being faithful to the Lord really isn't for the Lord's benefit; it's for our benefit. The more we grow in our walk with the Lord, the less we see of ourselves, and the more we see of Him.

Reflect on how you could be more faithful to the Lord in a present circumstance.

What happens when tragedy strikes? What should our response be to:

…the loss of a student?
…a coworker who is diagnosed with cancer?
…any type of abuse - child abuse, emotional abuse, physical abuse, etc?
…a student who undergoes illness?
…the loss of a teaching position?
…losses due to natural disasters like floods, fires, earthquakes, etc.?
…personal sickness, loss, or heartache?

Unfortunately, we all face tragedies, so we need to know how we are supposed to respond with faithfulness.

Although it's an oft-quoted verse, Romans 8:28 holds some vital truth for us when it comes to tragedy.

Look up Romans 8:28 and write it below.

Paul was reminding the Romans that ALL - A-L-L - things work together for our good and for the purpose that God had in mind for them.

It is easy in the good times to quote this verse and give it a hearty "Amen!" but when we are in the midst of tragedy, the last thing that we want to believe is that God allowed a difficult situation into our lives. How many times have you heard someone say - or perhaps you've said it yourself: how could a loving God allow *this* to happen?

"We take our circumstances for granted, saying God is in control, but not really believing it." - Oswald Chambers

The problem is that we are more me-focused rather than God focused. We forget that those two little words, "work together," in Romans 8:28 don't just mean that all the events of my life have to work together for good, but they also mean that the circumstances in my life and your life and my neighbor's life and your coworker's life and my student's life - they ALL come together to display God's glory. They work together for God's eternal purposes, not temporal, earthly ones.

"It is only a faithful person who truly believes that God sovereignly controls his circumstances." -Oswald Chambers

Let's pause a moment to think about what this does NOT mean:

It does NOT mean that God doesn't care about our heartache. Scripture is clear that "He heals the brokenhearted and binds up their wounds." (Psalm 147:3)

It does NOT mean that God finds joy or pleasure in watching His children suffer. Scripture is clear that "...though He cause grief, He will have compassion according to the abundance of His steadfast love; for He does not afflict from His heart or grieve the children of men." (Lamentations 3:32-33)

It does NOT mean that God allowed the tragedy in vain. We've seen this truth already. Scripture is clear that "...for those who love God all things work together for good, for those who are called according to His purpose." (Romans 8:28)

"We act as if the things that happen were completely controlled by people." -Oswald Chambers

When tragedy strikes, we often try to find someone or something to blame.

We blame stupid cancer.
We blame the food we ate or didn't eat.
We blame the drunk driver.
We blame parents.
We blame an administrator that doesn't get us.
We blame bad genes.
We blame drug and alcohol addiction.

Can you think of a time in your life when you tried to find someone or something to blame for a tragedy? Write or think about that time.

> "The goal of faithfulness is not that we will do work for God, but that He will be free to do His work through us. God calls us to His service and places tremendous responsibilities on us. He expects no complaining on our part and offers no explanation on His part. God wants to use us as He used His own Son." -Oswald Chambers

If God wants to use us as He used His own Son, we must think about the climax of His Son's life - the Cross. Jesus came to die in our place and "for the joy that was set before Him endured the cross." (Hebrews 12:2) Jesus was willing to suffer in order that we might have salvation. He was willing to allow His Father to work in and through Him to accomplish His purposes. Jesus was willing to bear the weight of all our sin, but also all of our suffering and pain. Were it not for sin that we can trace all the way back to the Fall in Genesis 3, we would have no suffering. Because sin entered the world, Jesus came willingly to shoulder the weight of all the sin, suffering, and sorrow we would otherwise have to shoulder alone.

Isaiah 53:4-5 says, "Surely He has borne our griefs and carried our sorrows; yet we esteemed Him stricken, smitten by God, and afflicted. But He was pierced for our transgressions; He was crushed for our iniquities; upon Him was the chastisement that brought us peace, and with His wounds we are healed."

So let's go back to our original question: what should our response be when tragedy strikes? Well, first, we need to remember that tragedies come in all shapes and sizes. We started today by mentioning some pretty hefty ones, but what about those speeding ticket trials? or fender-bender trials? or washing machine died trials? You see, our response to the small trials shapes our response to the bigger trials. We have to "practice" responding properly to the smaller ones, so that our response muscles are conditioned for the moments that the bigger trials hit.

DAY 3

shaken

http://bit.ly/wewillnotbeshakenfruited

The way that we respond to trials - big or small - goes back to those roots. If our roots are shallow, our response will be weak. We will be easily shaken by tragedy. If our roots are deep, our response will be strong. We will shakan - remember that word from yesterday? Let's determine to be people with deep roots. People who remember that even in the face of tragedy: Our God is sovereign. Our God is loving. Our God is in full control. Our God has a purpose for pain. Our God is faithful.

93

DaY 4   CULtiVate FaithfULness

This week has been filled with some pretty heavy topics. Trials, tough spots, and tragedies, oh my!! ☹😳 But if we go back to Day 1 where we started, we will remember that we began with God's faithfulness to us. Understanding His faithfulness in turn allowed us to unpack the response we should have to His faithfulness and the benefits we reap from being found faithful. We first needed to see the characteristic of faithfulness in the Ever Faithful One so that we could know what it would look like to imitate Him.

Before we get too far, glance back at Day 1 of this week and write the first definition of faithfulness below.

[ ]

Let's jump back to the Galatians in order to understand this Fruit of the Spirit. We need to ask ourselves: why was Paul wanting the Galatians to display the fruit of faithfulness?

Remember the situation that was taking place in Galatia that we discussed in Week 1? Galatia was in desperate need of Christians who were going to be faithful. Faithful to the Gospel. Faithful to Jesus. Faithful to Paul. Faithful to each other.

Look up and read 2 Timothy 2:1-2.

What was Paul asking Timothy to entrust and commit to faithful men?

[ ]

In order for the true Gospel to be spread in Galatia and to the surrounding areas, Paul needed Timothy to train faithful men, who would willingly stand out from the crowd in order to take a stand for Christ. These men needed to adorn their lives with the Gospel.

What would it look like for us to adorn our lives with the Gospel?

[ ]

Day 4 Cultivate Faithfulness

What does it look like to be faithful in our jobs as teachers?

- Our students and their parents should be able to trust that we are going to do what we say we are going to do.
- Our administrators should be able to trust that we will accomplish the tasks that are given to us - even the mundane ones. **#reports #curriculummaps #PDs**
- Our coworkers should be able to trust that we will have their backs, not throw them under the bus.

What does it look like to be faithful to our families?

- We should honor our time with them by giving them our undivided attention.
- We should love them despite their human frailties...because we have ours, too. **#weaintperfect**
- We should serve them by making them a priority.

What does it look like to be faithful in our church?

- We should be committing our time and service to a local body of believers.
- We should not think that the church is there to serve us and our agenda. **#mystyleofmusic #preachingmyway #wearwhatiwear**
- We should be working to create an environment that fosters outreach, not in-reach. **#thatsmypew**

It's your turn now. On the next page, we've given you four boxes. Fill them in with areas in your personal life where you need to cultivate faithfulness. Your categories may be: faithfulness to your marriage, your sister, your children, your parents, your class, etc. List some specific ways that you will strive to be more faithful in those areas.

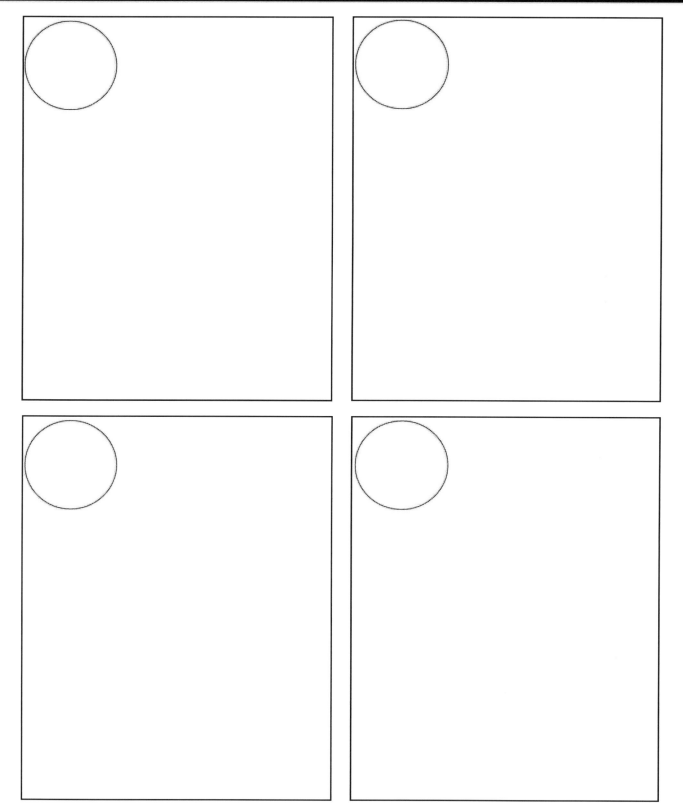

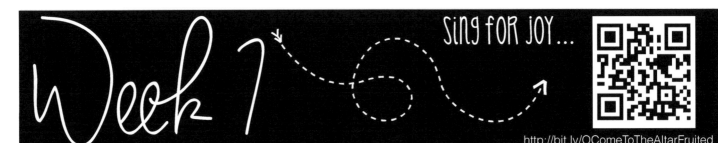

SCRIPTURE MEMORY: "Abide in me, and I in you. As the branch cannot bear fruit by itself, unless it abides in the vine, neither can you, unless you abide in Me. I am the vine; you are the branches. Whoever abides in Me and I in him, he it is that bears much fruit, for apart from Me you can do nothing." John 15:4-5

Kindergarten is the season for learning self control. By nature, five and six year olds are just rather impulsive. **#canigetanamen** Consequences are not what they think about. They do or say whatever their impulsive little selves think, and whatever follows, well...it just follows.

One little friend of mine seemed to need a little extra schooling in this self control department...

• It was not unusual to find him sprinting around the room at any given time. Middle of math time? No problem. Time for a run! 😬

• It was not unusual to find him closing himself in a container for fun. Middle of book buddy time? No problem. Time for silliness! 🤪

• It was not unusual to find him spewing whatever came to his mind to whoever was listening. Middle of reading time? No problem. Time for removing all filters...or never mind...the filter was never there to begin with... 😜

Now, don't get me wrong, this little guy was precious. He was loving and had a love of life that was incomparable. He just needed a filter - a filter for words and for actions.

Somehow I don't think my little buddy is the only one who struggles with self control. Somehow I think most adults struggle with this trait in many areas, too.

Why is self control important in a kindergartener? Because part of what I am teaching them is social interaction skills. If my goal is to help them develop skills that will follow them into adulthood, they for sure need to know how not to interrupt someone every time they have something to say. Running around a room randomly during a meeting may not go over so well either. 😂

We are going to discover a similar reason for honing our self control this week. Let's get ready to dive into this last week together as we learn the reason for practicing self control...it may not be quite what you think.

Fill in the blank.

"But the fruit of the Spirit is love, joy
peace, patience, kindness, goodness,
faithfulness, gentleness, and _____ ."
Galatians 5:22

self control
(egkrateia)
noun

1. self-control (the
virtue of one who
masters his desires
and passions, esp.
his sensual
appetites)
2. occurs 4 times

Can you believe it? We are embarking upon our last
week's journey together! Where has the time gone??🫣

Before we get too swept up in counting down our
minutes together, let's take a trip back in time. We
need to go alllllll the way back to Week 1 of our study.
Day 4 to be exact. Do you recall our cute, little girl
with the LOVE umbrella? Did you happen to notice
anything missing? Flip back now and see if you can
spot the missing fruit...

Did you find it? Did you make Sherlock Holmes proud? 😎

Self control was indeed the missing link! Now, the real question is: do you know why?
Take a guess...it's okay to be wrong. We tell our kids that all the time, right?

If love is the umbrella, self control is the book end. Self control is the culmination of all of the Fruit of the Spirit. In other words, in order to walk out the other eight fruit, we must practice self control in many areas.

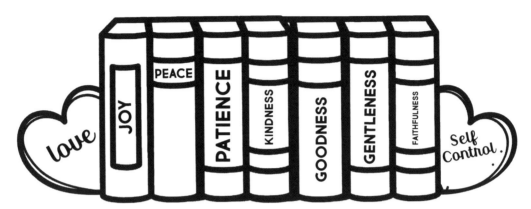

The word that Paul uses for self control is only used a handful of times in Scripture. In order to understand what he meant by this word and what his intention was for the Galatians and for us, let's visit another one of his letters.

Turn to 1 Corinthians 9 and read verses 24-27.

When we have a fitness goal in mind, we have to set up a fitness plan. Maybe we decide what our workouts are going to look like. Maybe we set up a meal plan. We utilize self control in order to get to our goal. Paul is saying that the Christian walk is much like running a race.

While a runner is after a prize that is perishable - a gold medal or a ribbon - Christians are running a race that will culminate in Heaven where imperishable crowns will be handed out and then laid at Jesus' feet. For this earthly race that has been set before us, we must have a "fitness plan" that helps us reach our goal, and that plan is going to include an awful lot of self control.

So let's first answer this: what is our goal? Let's hear it straight from Jesus' mouth.

Turn to Matthew 28:19-20. What were Jesus' last words to His disciples?

So our goal, then, is to bring others to Christ.

We are to let our **lives** speak for Jesus.
We are to let our **actions** speak for Jesus.
We are to let our **words** speak for Jesus.

In order for our lives, actions, and words to ooze Jesus, we certainly need a meal plan that includes a steady and hefty diet of God's Word. His Word in us helps us to bear the fruit that we've studied the past several weeks. Bearing that fruit is where self control comes in as well...

When we are tempted not to be loving because someone is frankly just getting on our last nerve 😑 **#stopclickingthatpen #mustyoukeeptalking #youwannaarguewithme**, our steady diet of God's Word comes to the rescue and helps us to speak truth to ourselves. It reminds us of our goal, first and foremost. It also reminds us that "love is patient." (1 Corinthians 13:4) When our "food" kicks in, self control activates. We control our desire to lash out and instead, choose to love as Jesus loves because we want our words and actions to speak for Jesus.

When we are tempted to be negative rather than joyful because **#iwantitmyway**, our steady diet of God's Word reminds us, "'For my thoughts are not your thoughts, and your ways are not my ways.' This is the LORD'S declaration." (Isaiah 55:8) When that "food" kicks in, self control activates, and we control our desire to let our momentary circumstances disrupt our joy because we remember our goal: to let others see Jesus.

When we are tempted to let unrest settle in because...well, **#anxiety #thefutureisscary #thepresentisscary**, our steady diet of God's Word reminds us that we can have "the peace of God, which surpasses all understanding and [can] guard our hearts and minds in Christ Jesus." (Philippians 4:7) When that "food" kicks in, self control activates and reminds us that our God is Sovereign even during the times that feel scary and chaotic to us. We remember our goal once again, too. We want people to see Jesus in us. We want them to see that in the midst of very real situations that bring very real fear into our hearts, we have a God Who cares and Who can bring peace in the midst of the most turbulent of waters.

Self control helps us to restrain our natural tendencies. We were born sinners. It is only by God's grace and His gift of the Holy Spirit that our once rebellious hearts begin to be shaped and fashioned into hearts that look like His and respond like His.

On the next page, pick a fruit...any fruit! Explain how self control can help you exhibit that fruit in your life. For an extra challenge, find a verse that you can add into your "meal plan" that demonstrates God's Truth about the fruit you picked.

VERSE
Challenge

Let's take a peek into a kindergarten classroom for a second...

Why are you wrestling with your friend? This is not WWE!

Why are you turning cartwheels right now? You are going to hit your friend. Centers, now!

You don't like this center and don't want to do it? I'm sorry. You need to do it.

You cannot uninvite Johnny from your birthday party. That is not loving. That is not kind.

Shew! Babies need some self control!

In a middle or high school classroom...

You purposely posted something rude on Instagram to get back at your classmate who didn't pick you for a group project? That is unkind.

Arguing with me over this math problem answer is not going to change the fact that your answer is wrong. You're being disrespectful.

Copping an attitude with me because I had to give you a zero since you didn't complete your homework is not okay.

Throwing your book across the room because you're mad is not acceptable.

Gah! Big kids need self control! 😳

Self control in actions seems to be something that kids struggle with maybe a little more than most adults - yes, there are exceptions, of course. Hopefully we aren't still wrestling on the carpet or turning cartwheels through our classrooms instead of teaching! **#lol** 😂

As adults, our self control struggles are a little different. We struggle more with thoughts and words usually.

WATCH YOUR
thoughts,
THEY BECOME
Words.

Self control really begins in our thoughts. Have you ever heard the saying, "if you don't control your thoughts, they will control you"? So much truth in that statement. Let's see what Paul has to say about thoughts.

Turn to 2 Corinthians 10:5b. Write the second half of the verse below.

[ ]

Paul also speaks about thoughts in Philippians 4:8. Turn there and list below the 8 things he says we should think on.

1. _____

2. _____

3. _____

4. _____

5. _____

6. _____

7. _____

8. _____

We, as women, have a really hard time with this very verse. We tend to go to "worst case scenario" thoughts immediately. We overanalyze situations and work ourselves into a tizzy without even having the full picture. This is precisely what Paul is warning against. He would say...think on things that are true. Take what you know to be truth and think about that. Don't dwell on what you don't know to be true. Don't fill in the gaps when you're missing information. Don't think worst case scenario about someone; think of the truth that you know about them instead.

Below, we have given you one example where we as teachers may struggle to use self control in our thoughts. After our example, you try coming up with one example that perhaps you have struggled with in the classroom.

In the classroom...

...when a parent asks for a meeting, don't think worst case scenario and get your blood pressure sky high when you don't have all the information and don't even know why they want the meeting.

> ...

WATCH YOUR *Words,* **THEY BECOME** *Actions.*

While self control begins in our thoughts, our thoughts are quickly turned into words.

Turn to Psalm 141:3 and write the verse below.

We don't know about you, but we desperately need the Lord to put a guard over our lips! Some days more than others!

My, Bethany's, middle schoolers sometimes ask me for duct tape. They just know when they're struggling to control their little mouths some days, and for whatever reason, tape on their lips is their favorite personal fix.

The more that we learn to use self control with our thoughts and take our sinful thoughts captive, the less those not-so-great thoughts will escape from our lips.

Let's see what our friend, Paul, has to say about controlling our words.

Turn to Ephesians 4:29. What kind of words should NOT come out of our mouths?

What kind of words SHOULD come out of our mouths?

Words are also tough for women...because let's face it...we LOVE to talk!
But watching what we say is important. Our words should build others up. Our words should sound like Jesus.

In the classroom...

...when we're congregating with other teachers - whether at lunch, in the workroom, meeting for coffee, etc. - we often struggle to speak up when others are talking about a student, coworker, parent, or administrator in a way we know is not building them up.

...

WATCH YOUR

Actions

THEY BECOME

Your character.

If self control begins in our thoughts and our thoughts eventually become words, those words will eventually creep into our actions. Yikes! 😳

Remembering back to the beginning of this day, we said that as we grow into adults, we don't struggle with the same kind of actions that our students do...but we still struggle. Our actions just look a little different.

Let's say that we have over-talked a particular situation with a close friend. Our emotions are raging. Rather than letting ourselves calm down, rather than taking our thoughts captive, we talk and talk and talk about it, and then BAM! We go and confront the other person, knowing that the confrontation will most likely do nothing to solve the problem but rather simply cause divisiveness and anger and hurt feelings. That is a situation where our actions lacked self control.

To use self control in a situation like that would be to go to the Lord in prayer over the situation. It would be letting ourselves calm down and "sleep on it," as we like to say, before we act on anything. Nine times out of ten, the next day, we aren't as stirred up, so our boldness decreases, and we realize the confrontation is useless for anything other than being divisive.

For whatever reason, it has also become a popular action to post on social media as a way of airing our dirty laundry. **#nobodywantstoseethat** 😳 We post negative thoughts about teaching, students, Mondays, government. Ain't nothin' gonna be solved on social media. In fact, what those posts do is make our thoughts more negative, which then affects our words, which then affects our actions...the whole lack of self control cycle starts again.

As our quote above reminds us, our actions become our character. People know us by our actions. Even a child, Proverbs 20:11 tells us, is known by his or her actions. And back to our goal - if we want people to see Jesus in us, our actions need to reflect Him.

WATCH YOUR *thoughts*
THEY BECOME WORDS

WATCH YOUR *words*
THEY BECOME ACTIONS

WATCH YOUR *Actions*

THEY BECOME YOUR CHARACTER

We don't know about you, but sometimes when we read the analogies in Scripture, we get a little lost. Shepherding? Yea, uh, that's a no from us...never done it. Blacksmith work? Um, yea, that's a no, too...never been there or done that. Grafting? Um...huh? What's that??😄

You see, Jesus was a master teacher. He fit his analogies and lessons to his audience. He knew that his audience knew about shepherding, knew about blacksmithing, and knew about grafting.

We, on the other hand, have to do a little extra study on these topics that make us go, "Huh?"

Before we go there, turn to John 15. It's is one of the most **#rootfilled** and **#fruitfilled** passages in all of Scripture. Read verses 1-17. We'll meet you back right here.

This **#fruitedlyfe** has never been about us, y'all. It's always been about Him...from day 1.

So let's go back to the beginning.

In John 15:1, what does He call Himself?

Same verse. Different question. What does He call the Father?

If Jesus is the Vine and His Father is the Vinedresser, then as verse 2 says, we are the branches. At the moment of salvation, we were grafted onto the Vine.

Fun educational learning opportunity for ya...if you want to know what grafting is, go check out YouTube for 4,378,293,438,942,739 videos. 😂 But for real, y'all, there are endless numbers of videos! It's actually a pretty cool process with a lot of application to this passage.

Basic idea of grafting, though, when farmers or vinedressers want to increase fruit production or change the type of fruit they are producing, they take branches from a tree or vine that they like and put them into the trunk or vine that is lacking. They do this by cutting into the trunk or vine and essentially "gluing" the branch into place. In a short period of two years, the tree with its new branches will bear the new fruit just as strongly as the original branches. The vine has an even quicker turn around time, showing growth in as little as one month.

So the purpose of grafting is simply to get a tree or a vine to bear more fruit and to bear the kind of fruit that the farmer or vinedresser desires.

Hear an application? We do, too! 😎 Our job is to bear fruit. It's all about that **#fruitedlyfe** y'all!

Listen to what Andrew Murray has to say about being the branches:

> You need to be nothing more. You need not for one single moment of the day take upon you the responsibility of the Vine. You need not leave the place of entire dependence and unbounded confidence. You need, least of all, to be anxious as to how you are to understand the mystery, or fulfill its conditions . . . The Vine will give all and work all . . . You need be nothing more than a branch.
> Only a branch!

Is it just us, or does that help you breathe easier? Insert sigh of relief! 😎

Let's revisit John 15:4. Notice the preposition that's mentioned twice the first sentence of that verse. Write that first sentence below and circle the preposition.

If you've been wondering this whole study long how you were going to produce the Fruit of the Spirit in your life, that little preposition is the answer. You must be consistently growing IN and rooted IN Christ, the Vine.

One word for ya'...grafted. Remember, when those branches are grafted, they are literally placed IN the trunk or IN the main vine. That's where they derive their life.

Being connected to the Life Source is what allows us not just to bear fruit, but to bear MUCH fruit as verse 5 says.

The one other process that helps a tree or a vine to bear fruit is pruning. When excess branches and leaves begin to get in the way, they can choke out the connection to the life source, the root. The same is true in our lives. Distractions can come. Things in our lives that were once good can absorb our time in a negative way. These will eventually separate us from the Life Source, Jesus, if He does not prune our lives of those things.

Pruning hurts. How can something be cut off from you be pleasant?? Let's think of some instances of pruning...

...not getting the job you wanted.
...a relationship ending suddenly.
...financial strains.

Think about a specific time in your life where you know the Lord was pruning you in order to set you up to bear more fruit for Him.

We always must remember that bearing fruit is our assignment. Verse 8 tells us that the Father is glorified when we bear fruit. The fruit that we bear is FOR Him, not us. As we've seen the past 6 1/2 weeks together, the point of our fruit is to draw others to Jesus.

Read verse 16. What has the Father appointed us to do?

In the same verse, we are told that not only should we bear fruit, but that our fruit should abide...it should live. It shouldn't rot and die; it should live. All the time. In all that we do, our fruit - in all its sweet glory - should be reflecting the Vine and the Vinedresser.

One last note Jesus leaves us, and oh what a sweet reminder it is. 😎 Write verse 17 below.

Remember why Paul was telling the Galatians to bear this fruit? He wanted them to stand out in a culture of ungodliness.

You know why we are to bear fruit? So that we love one another. Loving one another makes us stand out in a world that desperately needs Jesus.

So now, what do we do? We...

Are you *feelinfruity* yet?

We have now come to the end of our seven-week journey together.

We have laughed.
We have cried.
We have been pruned.
We have been convicted.
We have cultivated roots.
We have dug deeper.
We have learned to live **#thefruitedlyfe**.

…and now it is time for us to part ways, so we can go and bear fruit.

Before we go, we want to leave you with our final greetings - letters from us to you.

When you've finished reading our letters, we'd like you to write a letter, too. But this letter is a letter from you to future you. Think of it as a pick-me-up letter. A letter you'll re-read in the coming days when things are hard and you need some encouragement. Remind yourself of the things you've gleaned from our seven-week journey together. Remind yourself of truths that God has revealed to you from His Word.

We've given you a blank page for this letter if you'd like to tuck it away inside this study. You may also decide that you want to write it on your own paper and tuck it away inside an envelope somewhere just for future you. Or maybe you have a journal where you'd like to keep it. **#youdoyou**

So…without further ado…

#THEFRUITEDLYFE

One of my favorite children's books is *The Oak Inside the Acorn* by Max Lucado. To give a brief synopsis of the story…

Little Acorn began his journey attached to his mother, The Oak Tree. Little Acorn was scared to leave his mother and worried what his purpose in life was going to be. Each day, Little Acorn grew heavier and heavier. Eventually, he became too heavy to hang onto his mother, and he fell to ground. As he was falling, his mother called out to him, "Just be the tree that God made you to be!" Little Acorn was unsure what this statement meant to him as a small acorn. He was swept away by the farmer's truck and was accidentally planted in an orange grove. As he began to grow, he wondered if he would produce oranges like his friends in the orange grove. He remembered his mother telling him, "Just be the tree that God made you to be." The farmer noticed the tiny oak tree in the orange grove and removed him and planted him in the yard near his home. While planted in the yard, he began to wonder if he would bloom like the flowers. He didn't understand what kind of tree God made him to be. Eventually, he grew as tall as the farm house. Eventually, the farmer's daughter began to play under the tree and swing on the swing that was held by the now strong oak tree's branches. The tall oak tree fell in love with the little girl as she played under him during the summer months. As the girl grew older, she played less and less and sat more and more. One day, the girl looked sad and wondered aloud at what plan God had for her life. As the Big Oak Tree wondered how he could help the young girl, he remembered what his mom had told him as a small acorn. The Oak Tree shook his branches and let one of his acorns fall. When the acorn hit the lap of the girl, she remembered that the oak tree once started out as a small, little acorn. She was amazed at how the once small acorn was now a big oak tree. Little Acorn had become the tree that God made him to be. He realized that he needed to let go and become the tree that God made him to be.

Sweet teacher friends, as each and every student enters into the world of education, they come to us as small baby acorns. As the year progresses, they turn into baby trees that need cultivating and pruning each school year. Little Oak Tree thought he would bear oranges, but he didn't bear oranges. He thought he would produce flowers, but he didn't produce flowers. Our students may have many ideas of what they would like to be when they grow up, but it is our job and role as teachers to help them grow into the trees that God has made them to be.

As Little Oak became Big Oak, his roots grew deeper and stronger. As his roots grew, he began to understand more about being the tree that God made him to be. We, as teachers, have an important job to help our students grow strong roots. We can't help our students grow strong roots without having strong roots ourselves. We must grow and strengthen our roots in Christ in order to pour into the lives of our students each school year.

I leave you with the same advice that Mama Oak told Little Acorn, "Just be the tree that God has made you to be." We must remember to let go of our own personal plans and be who God has made us to be. Be the teacher that God has made you to be: rooted in Him and bearing fruit. Live **#thefruitedlyfe.**

Bonnie Kathryn

I have struggled with what I should put on this page. What part of my heart should I share with you? What vulnerable spot should I open as I let you catch a glimpse? What would benefit you most yet glorify me least? What would put God in the spotlight rather than me or my past sin or my present struggles? I think what I want you to know is this...

For years, I struggled to be real with myself. I didn't want to admit that I, too, had faults and failures, sins and struggles. I was fine. Perfectionists are perfect after all, aren't we?? 😈 **#lies** I never wanted others to view me as less. I didn't want to lower someone's view of me if they discovered that I wasn't who they believed that I was.

The truth is - I am a sinner. The worst sinner of all. I tell my students often that I'd ALWAYS rather them lie to my face than lie behind my back and pretend to be nice to my face. "Just be real," I say, yet...do you know what I spent the majority of my life doing? Hiding things from others. Family included. Let me rephrase that - hiding sins from others. Hypocrite in the flesh. The worst of sinners. I told you.

Satan has a way of convincing you that you are fine. That you're on the right track. But in the same breath, in the same moment, he lures you into the trap of sin that sucks you down into its quicksand, and if you're not careful, it will claim your very life. Somehow the slippery slope of sin lands you in the very sins you never saw coming. "Not me!" We cry. "Not *that* sin!" But yes, you, and yes, *that* sin.

When I finally stared into the ugly face of my sin and got real with myself and admitted my faults to God, my thoughts immediately went to yet another lie from the enemy himself: *God can never use you now. You're disgusting.* And I believed that, too. *If people know I'm a sinner*, I thought, *they'll want nothing to do with me!*

Friends, can I tell you the beauty of truth? The truth is that God has ALWAYS been in the business of using real, dirty, rotten sinners. He has ALWAYS been in the business of redemption - taking what was messed up and making it whole again. His best messed up...and messed up BIG time! David. Paul. Peter. Just three prime examples while so many more exist.

Can I tell you another beautiful truth? When people discover you, too, have messed up, you are MORE relatable, not less! People look at you as...well...human. People understand that if God can transform *you*, He can transform them, too.

So what do I want you to know? I want you to know that you aren't beyond transformation. You aren't beyond redemption. If He could take my sinful, rebellious, hypocritical self and cleanse me and make me whole, you are not beyond where I was. As Corrie ten Boom said, "There is no pit so deep, that God's love is not deeper still." I don't care how deep you've dug that pit of sin you might be sitting in, His love is higher and deeper and wider and longer that any pit you could ever dig.

Look at yourself in the mirror. Go ahead. Meet your eyes. Now, speak truth to yourself. Tell yourself: He makes beautiful things. He *still* makes beautiful things out of us.

Friend, He loves you so much! He wants desperately to see you abiding IN Him. Let Him wrap you in His love as He allows His Spirit to work in you to produce His fruit in you, so that others may see something different in you - something that gives them a glimmer of hope for themselves and causes them to run headlong into the Savior's arms. After all, the Gospel is what it's all about. It's why we're here. It's the very reason He redeems. Let His transformation in you bring about His transformation of others as you live **#thefruitedlyfe** 😘

Until next time - you are loved!

Bethany

http://bit.ly/BeautifulThingsFruited   114

THE FRUIT OF JESUS' LIFE

Jesus showed love by...
dying on the Cross for us while we were still sinners. (Romans 5:8)

Jesus showed joy...
when He endured the Cross that was set before Him. (Hebrews 12:2)

Jesus offers peace to us...
when He tells us not to let our hearts be troubled or afraid because He has overcome the world. (John 14:27)

Jesus shows patience by...
allowing His kindness to lead us to repentance. (Romans 2:4)

Jesus shows His Kindness to us...
through the salvation He offers us because of His mercy. (Titus 3:4-5)

Jesus shows goodness by...
giving His good and perfect gifts to us. (Psalm 100:5; James 1:17)

Jesus shows faithfulness to us by...
remaining faithful even when we are faithless. (2 Timothy 2:13)

Jesus shows gentleness by...
offering us rest for our souls as we take on His gentle yoke. (Matthew 11:29)

Jesus shows self control by...
withholding His wrath from mankind right now so that more people can acknowledge Him as Lord. (Psalm 145:8)

Jesus lived #thefruitedlyfe

FReQUeNTLY ASKeD QUeSTIONS

I want to lead a group through this study. Is there a leaders' guide?

Yes! You may download the FREE leaders' guide at http://bit.ly/FruitedLeadersGuide

How should I map out my study week?

Begin your week by watching the weekly videos located on www.teachersintheword.com/fruited. There are four study days, one scripture memory day/day of rest, and one day for meeting with your Bible study group.

How do I get a cute #fruited t-shirt?

You may find the #fruited t-shirt on www.teachersintheword.com/fruited

Do you have any other Bible studies or devotionals?

Yes! We have written another Bible study on the book of Ephesians called *Grace Changes Everything*. You can find that study at www.teachersintheword.com/gce. We also send out monthly e-mail devotionals on the first day of each month. You may sign up for those emails at www.teachersintheword.com

How can I get connected with a community of Christian teachers?

We have a Facebook Group called Christian Teachers: Teachers in the Word. You may request access and join a community of other teachers that desire to grow in their walk with the Lord. We laugh, cry, and rejoice together as we support each other in this crazy life we call the **#teacherlife**. Each summer, we complete Bible studies together just like this one. Check it out at http://bit.ly/FBteachersintheword

Can I complete this study alone?

Yes, you can. You do not have to have a group to complete this study. However, we would encourage you to invite at least one of your friends to complete the study with you for accountability and fun. There are a group of teachers that are completing this study together online during the Summer of 2018. If you've found this study during that time, feel free to join that group of teachers in our Facebook Group: http://bit.ly/FBteachersintheword

What version of the Bible are you using?

We are using the English Standard Version (ESV). You do not need to purchase that version of the Bible in order to complete the study. You can answer all of the questions in the study without using the ESV. If you would like to use it for the study, you can download the YouVersion App on your phone or iPad and select ESV.

Scan me for more information and resources for #fruited.

TEACHERS IN THE *Word*

DeRouchie, Jason. *Love God with Your Everything.* 10 October 2013. March 2018. <https://www.desiringgod.org/articles/love-god-with-your-everything>.

George, Timothy. *The New American Commentary: Galatians.* Vol. 30. Nashville: B & H Publishing Group, 1994.

Platt, David and Tony Merida. *Christ-Centered Exposition: Exalting Jesus in Galatians.* Ed. David Platt, Daniel L. Akin and Tony Merida. Nashville: Holman Reference, 2014.

Unknown. *www.blb.org.* 2017. 30 April 2017. <https://www.blueletterbible.org>.

Various. *Commentaries.* 2018. 2018. <https://www.biblestudytools.com/commentaries/>.

Author Credits:
Bethany Fleming
Bonnie Hunter

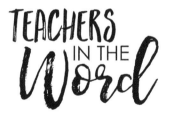

Made in the USA
Columbia, SC
02 May 2024

35162350R00067